# MAPS CHARTS GRAPHS

## United States Past and Present

## Level H

Project Editor: *Marty Geyen*
Editor: *Marty Green*
Editor: *Leslie Baranowski*
Project Design: *Mike Whipkey, Artful Communications*
Cover Illustration: *Jerry Harston*
Cover Design: *Francyne Abate Sepich*
Maps on pages 2-23, 28: *Sanderson Associates*
Maps on pages 30-43, 50-51, 62-63: *David Germon, Graphic Illustrator*
Graphs and Charts on pages 52, 54-70: *David Germon, Graphic Illustrator*
Photo Research: *Amy Van Hoose*

Photographs: *2, 67, The Granger Collection, New York; 5, D & I McDonald/The Picture Cube; 11, Michael Bertan/TSW-Click Chicago; 12, Richard Kosowski/Stockphotos, Inc.; 19, Charles McNulty/TSW-Click Chicago; 27, Dallas & John Heaton/TSW-Click Chicago; 33, Frank J. Staub/The Picture Cube; 41, Reims Photo 6851/Stockphotos, Inc.; 49, Stephen Marks/Stockphotos, Inc.; 61, UPI/Bettmann Newsphoto; 71, Modern Curriculum Press; 74, Culver Pictures.*

Maps on pages 24, 26, 46, and 48 from Deluxe Road Atlas & Travel Guide © Copyright 1989 by Rand McNally & Company, R.L. 89-S-193. Map on page 44 from Newsweek, June 27, 1988, National Oceanic and Atmospheric Admin.: The Dept. of Agriculture. Map on page 45 from Newsweek, June 9, 1986, Utah Geological and Mineral Survey.

Graph on page 53 from USA Today, August 2, 1988, © Copyright 1988, USA Today. Reprinted with permission.

Cartoon on page 72, "Nice timing." © Copyright 1988 by HERBLOCK in The Washington Post. Cartoon on page 73, Rogers, © Copyright 1988, Pittsburgh Press. Cartoon on page 74, Joseph Keppler. "Looking Backward," for Puck, January 11, 1893.

**Modern Curriculum Press**
An imprint of Pearson Learning
299 Jefferson Road, P.O. Box 480
Parsippany, NJ 07054–0480
http://www.pearsonlearning.com

ISBN 0-8136-2139-9

Printed in the United States of America

30   V011   16 15

# MAPS CHARTS GRAPHS

## United States Past and Present
## Level H

*Dale I. Foreman, Ph.D.*

*Sally J. Allen*
**Writer and Social Studies Consultant**

Modern Curriculum Press

# CONTENTS

| | | |
|---|---|---|
| **Lesson 1** | Finding Directions | 2-3 |
| **Lesson 2** | Using Map Scale | 4-5 |
| **Lesson 3** | Reading a Map Key | 6-7 |
| **Lesson 4** | Using a Letter-Number Grid | 8 |
| **Lesson 5** | Using Parallels and Meridians | 9-11 |
| **Lesson 6** | Finding Exact Locations on a Map | 12-13 |
| **Lesson 7** | Using an Atlas | 14-15 |
| **Lesson 8** | Reading Contour Maps | 16-17 |
| **Lesson 9** | Using Elevation Maps | 18-19 |
| **Lesson 10** | Comparing Map Projections | 20-21 |
| **Lesson 11** | Reading a Time Zone Map | 22-23 |
| **Lesson 12** | Using a Highway Map | 24-25 |
| **Lesson 13** | Using a City Map | 26-27 |
| **Lesson 14** | Reading an Historical Map | 28-29 |
| **Lesson 15** | Comparing Historical Maps | 30-31 |
| **Lesson 16** | Reading a Climate Map | 32-33 |
| **Lesson 17** | Reading a Weather Map | 34-35 |
| **Lesson 18** | Reading Special Purpose Maps | 36-37 |
| **Lesson 19** | Comparing Special Purpose Maps | 38-39 |
| **Lesson 20** | Interpreting an Historical Map | 40-41 |
| **Lesson 21** | Analyzing Map Data | 42 |
| **Lesson 22** | Finding the Best Location | 43 |
| **Lesson 23** | Analyzing Current Events Maps | 44-45 |
| **Lesson 24** | Finding the Best Route | 46-47 |
| **Lesson 25** | Planning a Trip | 48-49 |
| **Lesson 26** | Analyzing a Trend | 50 |
| **Lesson 27** | Solving a Land-Use Problem | 51 |
| **Lesson 28** | Reading a Circle Graph | 52-53 |
| **Lesson 29** | Comparing Circle Graphs | 54 |
| **Lesson 30** | Reading a Bar Graph | 55 |
| **Lesson 31** | Comparing Bar Graphs | 56 |
| **Lesson 32** | Reading a Double-Bar Graph | 57 |
| **Lesson 33** | Reading a Line Graph | 58 |
| **Lesson 34** | Reading a Double-Line Graph | 59 |
| **Lesson 35** | Interpreting Graphs | 60-61 |
| **Lesson 36** | Using a Map and a Graph Together | 62-63 |
| **Lesson 37** | Reading a Table | 64-65 |
| **Lesson 38** | Reading a Time Line | 66-67 |
| **Lesson 39** | Interpreting Time Lines | 68-69 |
| **Lesson 40** | Reading a Chart | 70-71 |
| **Lesson 41** | Reading a Political Cartoon | 72-73 |
| **Lesson 42** | Interpreting Historical Cartoons | 74-75 |
| **Glossary** | | 76 |
| **Answer Key** | | 77-80 |
| **Atlas** | | 81-92 |
| **Skills Index** | | Inside Back Cover |

# Finding Directions

**Objective:** to use a compass rose or direction arrow to find directions on a map

Maps give you many different kinds of information. One kind of information that nearly all maps show is direction. When you read a map, look for an arrow or other pointer to help you find directions.

The four most important directions are called the **cardinal directions.** Two of the cardinal directions are **north** and **south.** What are the other two?

1. ~~east~~        ~~West~~

The North Pole is the northernmost point on Earth. No matter where in the world you are standing, north is toward the North Pole. Likewise, the South Pole is the southernmost point on Earth. South is always toward the South Pole.

To describe directions that are not exactly north, south, east, or west, people combine these words. For example, the direction halfway between north and east is called northeast. The direction halfway between south and west is called southwest. Northeast, southeast, northwest, and southwest are **intermediate directions.**

Add all four intermediate directions to this diagram.

2.

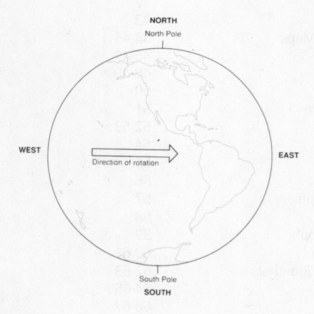

The drawing you have made is called a **compass rose.** Some maps have a compass rose to help you find all of these directions. Other maps have a pointer that shows only one direction, usually north. North is often at the top of the map—but not always! To be sure of directions, you should look for a north arrow or a compass rose.

Early navigators use placement of sun and stars to find directions.

**East** is the direction that Earth turns. It is the direction of the sunrise. **West** is the direction opposite east, and is the direction of the sunset.

If you know one direction, you can figure out the others. When you face north, south is straight behind you. East is to your right. West is to your left.

Use the map of Yellowstone National Park to answer the following questions.

## Yellowstone National Park

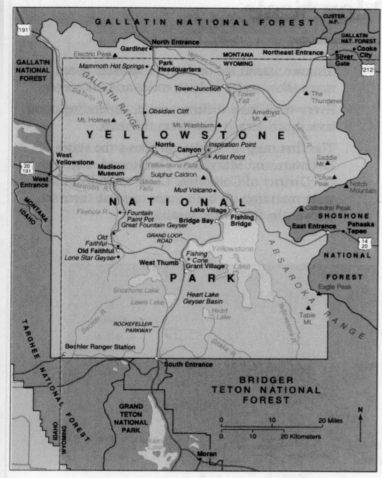

3. Find the north arrow on the map. Which edge of this map is the northern edge?

   a. left
   b. right
   c. top
   d. bottom

4. What state is on the northern boundary of Yellowstone National Park?

   a. Idaho
   b. Wyoming
   c. Montana
   d. Colorado

5. What national forests border Yellowstone on the west?

   a. Shoshone and Teton National Forests
   b. Gallatin and Targhee National Forests
   c. Targhee and Teton National Forests
   d. Gallatin and Shoshone National Forests

6. What direction do you travel to go from West Thumb to Old Faithful?

   a. north
   b. south
   c. east
   d. west

7. What river flows into Yellowstone Lake from the southeast?

   a. Snake River
   b. Bechler River
   c. Yellowstone River
   d. Madison River

8. Which one of these is located in the northwestern corner of the park?

   a. Bechler          c. Gallatin
   b. Silver Gate      d. Pahaska Tepee

9. What mountain lies northeast of Inspiration Point?

   a. Mt. Holmes
   b. Amethyst Mt.
   c. Saddle Mt.
   d. Sulphur Mt.

10. If you come into the park's west entrance at West Yellowstone, what is the shortest way to West Thumb?

   a. Go east to Madison Museum. Turn south to Old Faithful. Follow the Grand Loop Road east to West Thumb.
   b. Go east to Madison Museum. Turn northeast to Norris. Take the Grand Loop Road through Canyon and Bridge Bay to West Thumb.
   c. Go west on Highway 20 and 191. Turn north to Old Faithful. Follow the North Loop to West Thumb.
   d. Go west on Highway 20 and 191. Follow the Grand Loop Road east to West Thumb.

## Lesson 2

# Using Map Scale

**Objective:** to use the scale on a map to find and compare distances

Maps are **scale** drawings. Each inch on the map stands for a certain number of feet or miles on Earth's surface.

Most maps give you a scale bar to help you understand the distances shown on the map. To find out how far apart two places are, measure the distance between them with a ruler. Then use the scale bar to find how many miles that

distance stands for on Earth's surface. Some maps show scales in both miles and kilometers.

Every map has a different scale, depending upon how much area is shown on the map.

The first map in this lesson shows the states of Delaware and Maryland. The second map shows the District of Columbia. Look carefully at the scale markings on both maps and use them to answer the following questions.

**Delaware and Maryland**

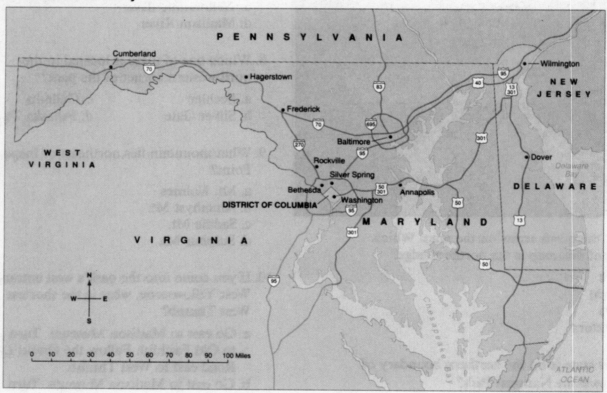

1. How many miles does the scale on the map of Delaware and Maryland represent?

   a. 10   b. 50   c. 20   (d.) 100

2. How far is it from Baltimore, Maryland, to Washington, D.C.?

   a. about 30 mi          (c.) about 50 mi
   b. about 20 mi          d. about 10 mi

*4*   *UNDERSTANDING THE TOPIC*

## The District of Columbia

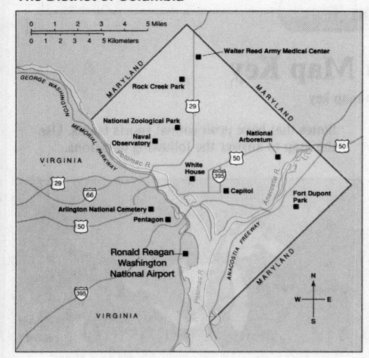

3. How long is the western border of Delaware?
   a. about 110 mi
   b. about 87 mi
   c. about 70 mi
   d. about 123 mi

4. What is the distance between Hagerstown, Maryland, and Wilmington, Delaware, in a straight line?
   a. about 85 mi
   b. about 145 mi
   c. about 35 mi
   d. about 115 mi

5. Suppose you wanted to drive from Frederick to Wilmington by interstate highway. If you took highways 70, 695 and 95, how far would you have to drive?
   a. about 105 mi
   b. about 135 mi
   c. about 65 mi
   d. about 150 mi

6. How many kilometers does the scale on the map of the District of Columbia represent?
   a. 5   b. 3   c. 15   d. 7

7. How many miles does the scale on the map of the District of Columbia represent?
   a. 5                 c. 15
   b. 3                 d. 7

8. About how many kilometers are there in 3 miles?
   a. 4                 c. 6
   b. 5                 d. 8

9. What is the distance from the Capitol to Fort Dupont Park?
   a. 10 mi             c. 5 mi
   b. 3 mi             d. 15 mi

10. What is the distance from the White House to the Walter Reed Army Medical Center?
    a. 1.5 mi           c. 15 mi
    b. 7.5 mi           d. 5.5 mi

11. On which map does an inch stand for more miles?

    DelaWare      Maryland

12. Which two cities are the farthest distance apart?
    a. Washington and Baltimore
    b. Frederick and Hagerstown
    c. Hagerstown and Washington
    d. Baltimore and Frederick

Visitors to Vietnam Memorial, Washington, D. C.

# Lesson 3

# Reading a Map Key

**Objectives:** to use the symbols and colors provided by a map key

Maps use **symbols** to present information. This map shows you the cities in the United States that have professional sports teams. Use the map to answer the following questions.

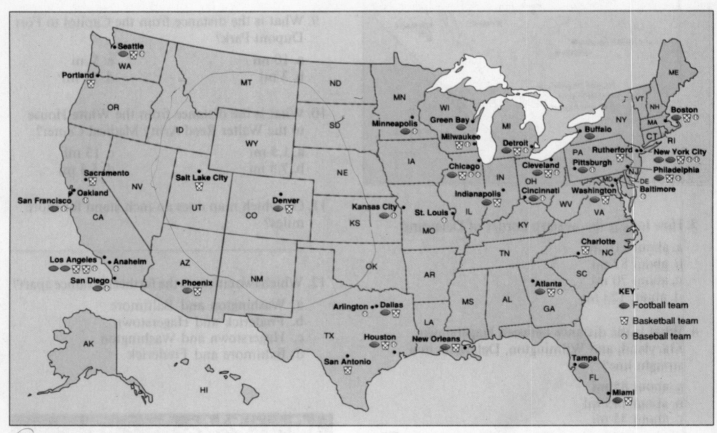

1. Which one of the following cities has a basketball team but not a football or a baseball team?

   a. Boston      c. Tampa
   b. Cleveland      d. Portland

2. What teams does Detroit have?

   a. baseball
   b. baseball and basketball
   c. baseball, football, and basketball
   d. basketball and football

3. Which state has the most teams?

   a. New York      c. California
   b. Pennsylvania      d. Texas

4. Which one of the following cities has a basketball team, a football team, and two baseball teams?

   a. Indianapolis      c. Houston
   b. Pittsburgh      d. Chicago

5. Which region of the country has the fewest professional sports teams?

   a. the eastern coast, from Maine to Florida
   b. the west central area, from Idaho and Nevada to Kansas, Nebraska, and the Dakotas
   c. the western coast, from Washington to California
   d. the southern border and coast, from Arizona to Alabama

This map gives you information about the **population density** of the United States.

**United States: Population Density**

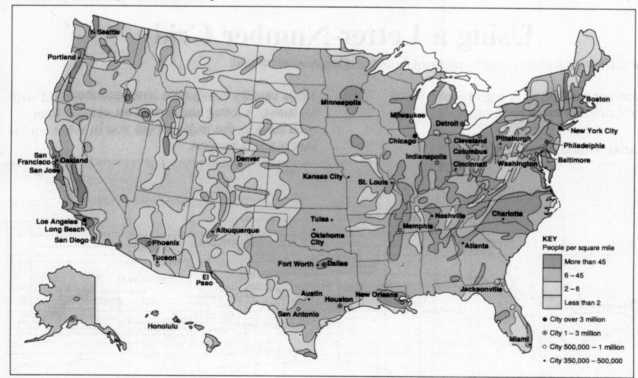

6. Which one of the following cities has the largest population?

   a. Washington, D.C.     c. Detroit
   b. Miami                d. Chicago

7. What is the largest city in California?

   a. San Diego        c. San Francisco
   b. Los Angeles     d. Long Beach

8. Which one of the following states has two cities of more than one million people?

   a. Pennsylvania    c. Texas
   b. New York        d. Michigan

9. What is the population of Philadelphia?

   a. 1-3 million people
   b. over 3 million people
   c. 500,000-1 million people
   d. 350,000-500,000 people

10. Which one of the following states has the lowest population density overall?

   a. Nevada         c. Arkansas
   b. Maine           d. Oregon

11. Which one of the following states has a population density of between 6 and 45 people per square mile over most of its area?

   a. North Dakota    c. Oregon
   b. Hawaii          d. Iowa

12. Which one of the following states has the highest population density overall?

   a. Georgia         c. Minnesota
   b. Massachusetts   d. Arkansas

13. Compare the two maps in this lesson. What is the largest city that has no professional sports team?

   a. Phoenix         c. Fort Worth
   b. Tulsa            d. Memphis

14. Write a short statement explaining how population density and sports teams seem to be related, based on these two maps.

   Higher population means more fans

# Lesson 4

# Using a Letter-Number Grid

**Objective:** to locate places on a map by using an index and a letter-number grid

Many maps are marked with a **grid** made up of two sets of lines that cross each other.

Maps usually combine a letter-number grid with an **index**. A letter and a number appear after each item in the index to tell you in what square that place is located.

**Manhattan Island, New York City**

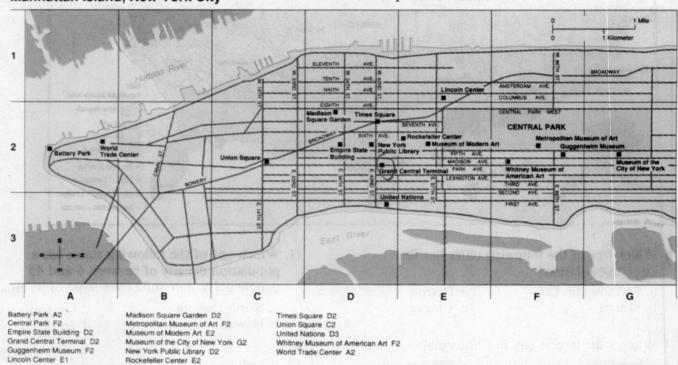

Battery Park A2
Central Park F2
Empire State Building D2
Grand Central Terminal D2
Guggenheim Museum F2
Lincoln Center E1

Madison Square Garden D2
Metropolitan Museum of Art F2
Museum of Modern Art E2
Museum of the City of New York G2
New York Public Library D2
Rockefeller Center E2

Times Square D2
Union Square C2
United Nations D3
Whitney Museum of American Art F2
World Trade Center A2

1. According to the index, in what section of the map will you find Grand Central Terminal?

   a. D-3   b. C-2   c. D-2   d. B-2

2. Find the terminal on the map and circle it.

3. On what street is the Whitney Museum of American Art located?

   a. Madison Ave.          c. Second Ave.
   b. Amsterdam Ave.        d. Fifth Ave.

4. At what corner is the New York Public Library?

   a. Eighth Ave. and Lexington Ave.
   b. Fifth Ave. and E. 42nd St.
   c. Broadway and E. 34th St.
   d. Central Park West and Columbus Ave.

5. Use the index to find each place listed below. Write the section of the map where it is located.

   a. World Trade Center _____ A2 _____
   b. United Nations _____ D3 _____
   c. Lincoln Center _____ E1 _____

6. Look for the direction indicator on the map. What direction would you be traveling if you went from Grand Central Terminal to Madison Square Garden?

   a. east   b. west   c. southeast   d. southwest

7. What would describe the most direct route from Times Square to the United Nations?

   a. south on E. 42nd St., then east on First Ave.
   b. east on 42nd St., then north on First Ave.
   c. north on Seventh Ave.
   d. south on Seventh Ave.

# Using Parallels and Meridians

**Objectives:** to use parallels and meridians to find places on a world map

Imagine a grid with one set of lines running north and south and another set running east and west. Picture this grid criss-crossing the whole world.

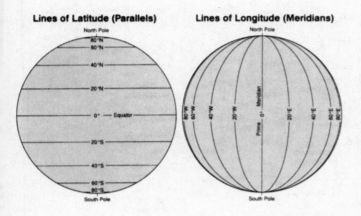

**Lines of Latitude (Parallels)**

**Lines of Longitude (Meridians)**

One set of lines is called **parallels of latitude.** They are called parallels because they are the same distance apart all the way around the world.

Look at the globe diagram showing parallels. Halfway between the North Pole and the South Pole, a special latitude line runs around the middle of Earth. What is it called?

1. _____ Ohuatrate _____

The **equator** is the starting point for measuring latitude. It is numbered 0° latitude. Latitude and longitude are measured in **degrees**, or parts of a circle, because Earth is round. The North Pole is the farthest point north of the equator. It has a latitude of 90° North. What is the farthest point south of the equator?

2. _____ South Pole _____

3. What is its latitude? _____ 90°S _____

The other set of lines is called **meridians of longitude.** Meridians are not parallel because they meet at the North Pole and the South Pole.

The starting place for measuring longitude is numbered 0° longitude. What is this line called?

4. _____ prim mullegh ___ spelling

Every meridian east of the **Prime Meridian** is east longitude. Every meridian west of the Prime Meridian is west longitude. Exactly half way around the world from the Prime Meridian is the meridian 180°. It is just as far east as west from the Prime Meridian, so it has no east or west label—only a number.

**Parallels and Meridians**

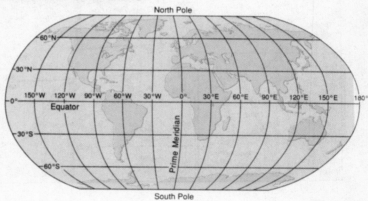

You can describe the location of any place on Earth just by saying which two lines cross there. To pinpoint a location, you use a pair of numbers. The first number tells the place's latitude, the second its longitude. These two numbers are called the **coordinates** of that particular place. For example, the coordinates 0°, 30° E locates a place in Africa on the map of the world.

This map of the United States has parallels and meridians to help you locate places. This map is also a **political map**. A political map shows the boundaries between states or countries. During the 1800s, when Americans were forming their states, they often set boundaries along parallels and meridians.

**The United States**

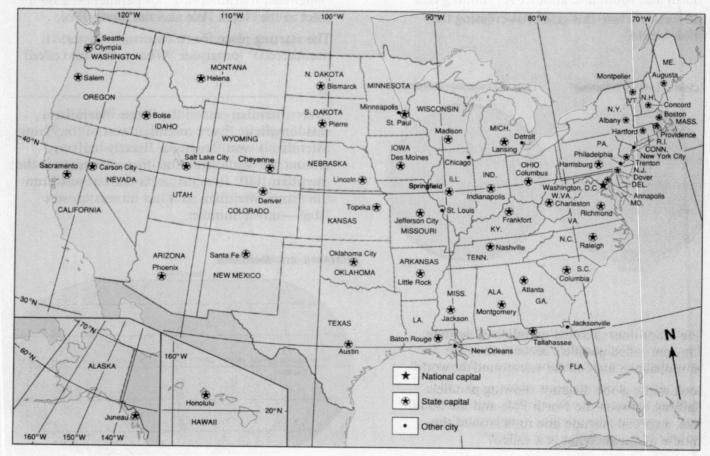

5. Which state's northern boundary is formed by the parallel 40° N?

   a. Kansas
   b. Pennsylvania
   c. Tennessee
   d. Nebraska

6. In which state is the place with the coordinates 30° N, 100° W?

   a. Florida
   b. Texas
   c. Arizona
   d. Iowa

7. Which set of coordinates describes a location in Illinois?

   a. 100° N, 40° W
   b. 40° N, 100° W
   c. 90° N, 40° W
   d. 40° N, 90° W

8. What city has the coordinates 30°N, 90°W?

   a. New York City
   b. Jacksonville
   c. New Orleans
   d. St. Louis

9. What direction would you travel to go from Chicago to Detroit?

   a. southeast
   b. southwest
   c. northeast
   d. northwest

10. What is the capital of the state of South Dakota?

    a. Pierre
    b. Bismarck
    c. Rapid City
    d. Sioux Falls

11. Which state has the northernmost latitude in the United States?

    a. Maine
    b. Minnesota
    c. Alaska
    d. Idaho

12. What direction would an airplane fly if it went from Seattle to Denver?

    a. northeast
    b. southeast
    c. northwest
    d. southwest

13. What do the latitude and longitude lines marked on the Alaska inset map tell you about its location?

    a. It lies 10° south of California.
    b. It lies 20° south of California.
    c. It lies 10° north of California.
    d. It lies 20° north of California.

14. This map does not show a line for <u>each</u> degree of longitude or latitude. To find degrees between the ones shown, you must estimate. Which set of coordinates describes the location of Washington, D.C.?

    a. 77° N, 41° W
    b. 39° N, 77° W
    c. 77° N, 39° W
    d. 41° N, 73° W

15. What parallel forms the northern boundaries of Arizona, New Mexico, and Oklahoma?

    a. 35° N
    b. 37° N
    c. 37° W
    d. 35° S

16. What meridian forms the western boundary of North Dakota, South Dakota, and part of Nebraska?

    a. 104° W
    b. 106° N
    c. 106° W
    d. 104° E

17. Which state capital is located on the eastern coast of the United States?

    a. Salem            c. Baton Rouge
    b. Boston           d. Denver

18. Which state has the southernmost latitude in the United States?

    a. Florida          c. Texas
    b. Hawaii           d. California

19. Identify the state capital located at each pair of coordinates.

    a. 40° N, 105° W _Denver_
    b. 40° N, 83° W _Cs(?)umoss_
    c. 40° N, 86° W _indiapols_
    _spelling_

20. Estimate the coordinates for each city to the nearest degree.

    a. Salem _123W_ _45N_
    b. Minneapolis _93W_ _5W_
    c. Carson City _120W_ _40N_
    d. Raleigh _81W_ _38N_

Lincoln's home in Springfield, Illinois has become a national historic site.

# Finding Exact Locations on a Map

**Objectives:** to use degrees and minutes of latitude and longitude to find specific locations

Each degree of latitude and longitude is divided into smaller units called **minutes** and **seconds**. Each degree is divided into 60 minutes. The symbol for minutes is ′. Each minute is divided into 60 seconds. The symbol for seconds is ″. A second is such a small measurement—about 106 feet—that it is rarely used on maps. However, many atlases give city locations in degrees and minutes.

Use the map of Hawaii to answer the following questions. Remember to estimate measurements that fall between degree lines.

**Hawaii**

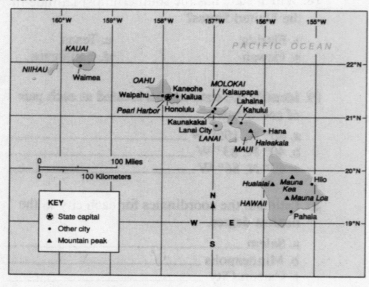

1. What is the latitude of the island of Kauai?

   a. 22° S
   b. 159°30′ N
   c. 22° N
   d. 159°30′ W

2. On what island is a place with the coordinates 19°30′ N, 155°30′ W?

   a. Oahu
   b. Hawaii
   c. Maui
   d. Kauai

3. Which two islands lie closest to 21° N latitude?

   a. Maui and Hawaii     c. Niihau and Maui
   b. Hawaii and Niihau   d. Maui and Molokai

4. What is the state capital of Hawaii?

   a. Lahaina            c. Hilo
   b. Kaneohe            d. Honolulu

5. What place has the coordinates 21°22′ N, 157°58′ W?

   a. Niihau             c. Pearl Harbor
   b. Lahaina            d. Mauna Loa

6. Which is the location of Honolulu?

   a. 21°19′ N, 157°52′ W
   b. 20°41′ N, 158°8′ W
   c. 23°35′ N, 158°50′ W
   d. 22°15′ N, 156°10′ W

7. What volcanic peak is located at 20°43′ N, 156°13′ W?

   a. Mauna Kea          c. Mauna Loa
   b. Haleakala          d. Hualalai

8. What is the approximate distance from Honolulu to Hilo?

   a. 50 mi              c. 200 mi
   b. 250 mi             d. 100 mi

The U.S.S. Arizona Memorial stands above the submerged battleship in Pearl Harbor.

Use this map of Alaska to answer the following questions. Remember to estimate measurements that fall between degree lines.

## Alaska

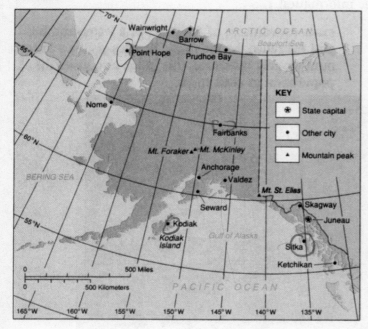

9. If you are at a point where 145° W crosses 55° N, where are you?

    a. in Skagway
    b. in the Bering Sea
    c. in the Pacific Ocean
    d. on Kodiak Island

10. What is the location of Juneau?

    a. 53°40′ N, 135°56′ W
    b. 57°30′ N, 133°18′ E
    c. 58°20′ N, 134°27′ W
    d. 59°05′ N, 137°42′ W

11. Which body of water is crossed by 70° N latitude?

    a. Gulf of Alaska
    b. Beaufort Sea
    c. Bering Sea
    d. Pacific Ocean

12. What place has the coordinates 70°20′ N, 148°20′ W?

    a. Barrow
    b. Prudhoe Bay
    c. Kodiak Island
    d. Fairbanks

13. How far is it from Nome to Juneau by air?

    a. about 500 mi
    b. about 1500 mi
    c. about 800 mi
    d. about 1100 mi

14. What is the location of Mt. McKinley?

    a. 63°04′ N, 151°0′ W
    b. 62°30′ S, 150°40′ W
    c. 68°20′ N, 153°30′ W
    d. 58°10′ N, 151°50′ W

15. About how far is it from Mt. McKinley to Wainwright by air?

    a. 1000 mi
    b. 550 mi
    c. 1500 mi
    d. 750 mi

16. Identify the place that lies closest to each pair of coordinates.

    a. 55°21′ N, 131°35′ W   Ketchikah
    b. 64°30′ N, 165°24′ W   Stagway
    c. 60°06′ N, 149°26′ W   Stlmil

17. Give the coordinates for each place to the nearest degree.

    a. Sitka   13ᴺN 58W
    b. Fairbanks   65N 156 W
    c. Kodiak   158N 68S
    d. Point Hope   69N 165W

18. Circle each city you located in question 17 on the map.

# Using an Atlas

**Objectives:** to use an atlas map and index to find basic information

An **atlas** is a book of maps. An atlas index, often called a **gazetteer**, lists all the map place names and the page number where you can find that place on a map. The index also gives either the exact coordinates of the place or a letter-number grid reference for the map. Besides giving a letter-number grid reference, this index also gives the population of each town.

**Florida**

**INDEX**

Boca Raton 49,505 .......... G5
Bradenton 30,170 .............. E4
Bristol 1,044 .................... C1
Browardale 7,409 ............. G5

Carol City 47,349 .............. G5
Chipley 3,330 ................... B1
Coral Gables 43,241 ........ G5
Cortez 3,821 .................... E4
Crestview 7,617 ............... B1
Cross City 2,154 .............. D2

Dade City 4,923 ............... E3
Davenport 1,509 .............. F3
De Land 15,354 ............... F2
Destin 3,672 .................... B1
Dunedin 30,203 ............... E3

Eagle Lake 1,678 ............. E3
Edgewater 6,726 ............. F2
Elfers 11,396 .................. E3
Englewood 9,633 ............. E4
Ensley 14,422 ................. A1
Eustis 9,453 ................... E2

Ft. Lauderdale 153,279 ..... G5
Fruitville 3,070 ................ E4

Geneva 1,120 .................. F3
Gifford 6,240 ................... F3

**KEY**
✳ State capital
• Other city
⊙ County seat

1. According to the index, in which grid square is Dunedin located?

   a. E-3   b. C-6   c. D-4   d. F-6

2. Find Carol City in the atlas index. Next locate Carol City on the map. Which county seat is south of Carol City?

   a. Ft. Lauderdale       c. Miami
   b. Dade City            d. Coral Gables

3. Which county seat is northwest of Gifford?

   a. Dade City            c. Wabasso
   b. Bradenton            d. Naples

4. Find Boca Raton. Along what body of water is Boca Raton located?

   a. Gulf of Mexico       c. Straits of Florida
   b. Atlantic Ocean       d. Florida Keys

5. What is the location of Naples?

   a. west of Browardale and north of Englewood
   b. west of Browardale and south of Englewood
   c. east of Browardale
   d. north of Browardale

6. Locate Fort Lauderdale. Which one of these cities is located northwest of Fort Lauderdale?

   a. Miami                c. Tampa
   b. Palm Beach           d. Naples

7. Locate Elfers. What major body of water is about 130 miles southeast of Elfers?

   a. Tampa Bay            c. Lake Okeechobee
   b. Florida Bay          d. Gulf of Mexico

Some atlas indexes use coordinates of latitude and longitude to describe locations of cities and towns. Use this atlas index and the map of Washington to answer the following questions.

### INDEX

Pasco 46°14′N 119°06′W
Pasig 14°33′N 121°05′E
Port Angeles 48°07′N 123°27′W
Port Orchard 47°32′N 122°38′W
Pullman 46°44′N 117°10′W
Puluo 36°11′N 81°30′E

Quatis 22°25′S 44°16′W
Quincy 47°14′N 119°51′W

Renton 47°30′N 122°11′W
Richland 46°17′N 119°18′W
Rioja 6°05′S 77°09′W

Seattle 47°36′N 122°20′W
Spokane 47°40′N 117°23′W
Stabroek 51°20′N 4°22′E

Tacoma 47°15′N 122°27′W
Tefle 5°59′N 0°35′E
Toppenish 46°23′N 120°19′W

Vervins 49°50′N 3°54′E
Viella 42°42′N 0°48′E
Villa Lia 34°07′S 59°26′W

Walla Walla 46°08′N 118°20′W
Wapato 46°27′N 120°25′W

Wenatchee 47°25′N 120°19′W
Wright 41°31′N 87°21′W

Yakima 46°36′N 120°31′W
Yasa 3°42′S 21°24′E

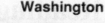

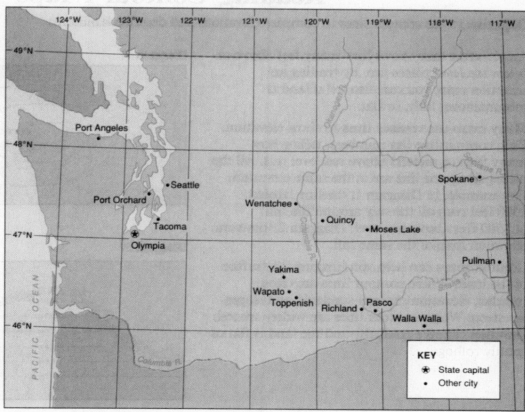

8. Find the city of Pullman in the index. Then use the coordinates to locate the city on the map and draw a box around it.

9. What city is located southwest of Pullman?
   a. Walla Walla       c. Moses Lake
   b. Spokane           d. Tacoma

10. Find the city of Seattle on the map without using the index. Write your estimate of the coordinates of Seattle to the nearest half a degree.

    47°N 122°W

11. Now look up the exact coordinates of Seattle in the index. Write these coordinates below.

    47°36 N      122°20W

12. Find the cities of Yakima and Wenatchee in the index. Then use the coordinates to locate the cities on the map. What direction would you travel to go from Yakima to Wenatchee by air?

    a. east   b. west   c. north   d. south

13. Find Wenatchee in the index and on the map. On what river is Wenatchee located?
    a. Columbia River       c. Spokane River
    b. Snake River          d. Saint Joe River

14. Find the coordinates of Walla Walla and Quincy in the index. Without looking at the map, name which city lies farther north.

    Port angeles

    Check your answer by locating both cities on the map.

# Reading Contour Maps

**Objective:** to use contour lines to compare elevations and describe landforms

An **elevation map** shows how many feet above or below sea level places are. By reading an elevation map, you can also tell if land is mountainous, hilly, or flat.

Many maps use **contour lines** to show elevation. Each contour line has numbers, telling how many feet (or meters) above sea level it is. All the places along one line are at the same elevation. For example, in Diagram 1, the line labeled 1500 feet runs all the way around the hill at 1500 feet above sea level. Diagram 2 shows an elevation map of the same hill.

Contour maps can help you imagine the surface of the land. Where contour lines are close together, elevation changes suddenly and slopes are steep. Where contour lines are widely spaced, elevation changes gradually and the land is flat or gently rolling.

**Diagram 1**

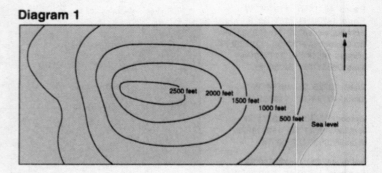

**Diagram 2**

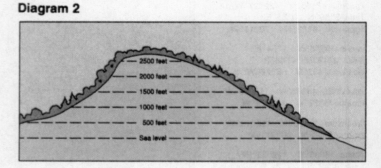

The contour map below shows an area of high lands and lowlands.

Use this contour map to answer the questions on the following page.

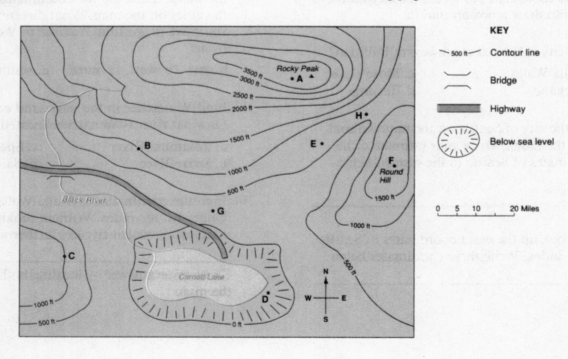

**KEY**

~500 ft~ Contour line

Bridge

Highway

Below sea level

0    5    10        20 Miles

1. What is the elevation of point B on the map?
   a. 0 ft
   c. 1000 ft
   b. 500 ft
   d. 100 ft

2. Which two points on the map are at the same elevation?
   a. points B and C
   b. points C and D
   c. points A and B
   d. points A and D

3. What is the elevation of point E?
   a. between 0 and 500 ft above sea level
   b. between 1000 and 1500 ft above sea level
   c. between 500 and 1000 ft above sea level
   d. between 1500 and 2000 ft above sea level

4. What is the highest point on the map?
   a. point D
   c. point B
   b. point F
   d. point A

5. What point on the map is below sea level?
   a. point F
   c. point H
   b. point D
   d. point G

6. Which point is near the base of a steep cliff?
   a. point C
   b. point G
   c. point H
   d. point B

7. What point lies northeast of Carnott Lake, at over 1500 feet?
   a. point F
   b. point B
   c. point E
   d. point H

8. At what elevation was the highway built?
   a. between 500 and 1000 feet
   b. between 1000 and 1500 feet
   c. between 500 feet and sea level
   d. between 1500 and 2000 feet

9. What is the elevation of point A?
   a. more than 3500 ft
   b. less than 3500 ft
   c. 3500 ft

10. At what elevation does Black River begin?
    a. about 3000 ft
    b. about 1000 ft
    c. about 500 ft
    d. about 2000 ft

11. How many feet higher is Rocky Peak than Round Hill?
    a. about 3500 ft
    b. about 2000 ft
    c. about 1000 ft
    d. about 1500 ft

12. How would the area look if you were standing at the southern edge of the map looking north?

    a.    b.    c.

13. Suppose that you hike from point C to point B to point G. Which statement best describes your hike?
    a. up a gradual slope, across a bridge, then up a steel hill
    b. down a gradual slope, across a bridge, up a gradual slope, then down a steep slope
    c. down a gradual slope, across a bridge, up a gradual slope, then down a gradual slope
    d. across a bridge, across flat land, then up a steep slope

14. Suppose you hike from point D to point F to point A. Tell about your hike on the lines below, describing it in the same way as the hike is described in question 13. Include all steps and the slope of the land.

    _____

    _____

    _____

    _____

    _____

    _____

# Using Elevation Maps

**Objectives:** to use elevation colors to compare elevations and describe landforms

Many maps use color to show elevation. Use the
elevation maps below to answer the following
questions.

## Tennessee: Elevation

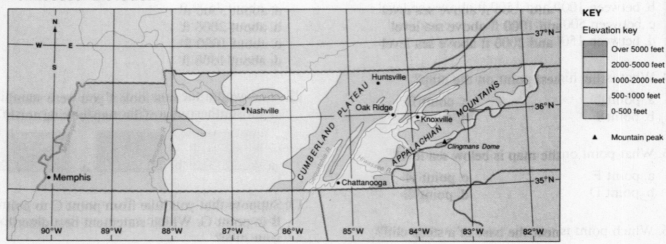

**KEY**

Elevation key

- Over 5000 feet
- 2000-5000 feet
- 1000-2000 feet
- 500-1000 feet
- 0-500 feet

▲ Mountain peak

## Colorado: Elevation

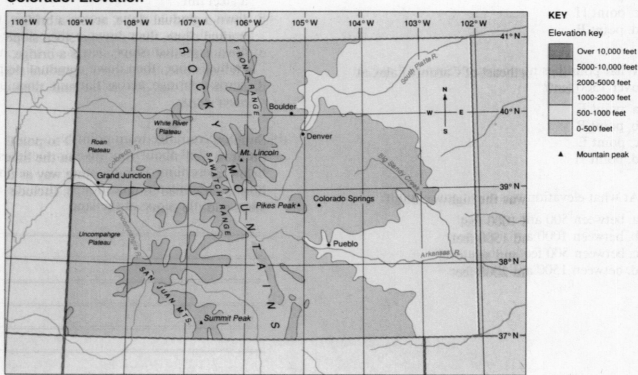

**KEY**

Elevation key

- Over 10,000 feet
- 5000-10,000 feet
- 2000-5000 feet
- 1000-2000 feet
- 500-1000 feet
- 0-500 feet

▲ Mountain peak

1. Which one of these colors shows the lowest elevation?

   a. yellow
   b. orange
   c. dark green
   d. light green

2. What color shows an elevation of 1700 feet above sea level?

   a. dark green
   b. light green
   c. orange
   d. yellow

3. What is the elevation of Memphis?

   a. between sea level and 500 feet
   b. between 500 and 1000 feet
   c. between 1000 and 2000 feet
   d. between 2000 and 5000 feet

4. What is the elevation of Denver?

   a. between sea level and 500 feet
   b. between 500 and 1000 feet
   c. between 5000 and 10,000 feet
   d. above 10,000 feet

5. Where in Tennessee are the highest elevations located?

   a. along the Mississippi River
   b. on the eastern border in the Appalachian Mountains
   c. between the Tennessee River and the Cumberland Plateau
   d. in the Cumberland Plateau

6. Which one of these cities is located on the flattest land?

   a. Chattanooga
   b. Knoxville
   c. Nashville

7. Which one of the following places has the highest elevation?

   a. Cumberland Plateau
   b. Appalachian Mts.
   c. Roan Plateau
   d. Rocky Mts.

8. Which one of the following places is a mountain range?

   a. Sawatch
   b. Chickamauga
   c. Uncompahgre
   d. Big Sandy

Clingmans Dome, Tennessee's highest peak in the Great Smokies

9. What mountain is located at 38°51′ N, 105°03′ W?

   a. Mt. Lincoln
   b. Pike's Peak
   c. Colorado Springs
   d. Summit Peak

10. Which description best fits the state of Tennessee?

   a. rugged hills and valleys in the west and gently rolling plains in the east
   b. a broad, high plateau in the east, rising steeply to mountains over 10,000 feet in the west
   c. broad lowlands in the west, rising to hills and mountains in the east
   d. level plains and lowlands in the south, with a ridge of highlands in the north

11. Based on information on the map, in what direction does the Uncompahgre River flow?

   a. southwest
   b. northwest
   c. southeast
   d. northeast

12. Which one of the following statements correctly compares Tennessee and Colorado?

   a. Eastern Tennessee has a higher elevation than eastern Colorado.
   b. Most of Tennessee has a higher elevation than Colorado.
   c. Only the highest mountains in Tennessee are as high as the lowest elevations in Colorado.
   d. Both Colorado and Tennessee have broad stretches of lowland river valleys.

# Comparing Map Projections

**Objectives:** to identify several map projections and compare their features

Earth is a sphere, and so the most accurate way to show Earth's surface is with a globe. On a globe, both the sizes and the shapes of continents and oceans are shown accurately. No flat map of the whole Earth can be as accurate as a globe.

To make a flat picture of the round Earth, map makers must change sizes and shapes of lands and oceans. These changes are called **distortion**. All maps have some distortion. The more of

Earth's surface a map shows, the more it has been flattened and distorted. Maps of the whole world show the most distortion. Maps of small areas show the least.

Map makers have tried many ways of drawing Earth. These drawings are called **projections**. Below are some of the most often used projections. You can see how each projection shows the whole world and North America.

## Mercator Projection

The Mercator Projection shows the true shapes of land areas. However, the sizes are distorted. Land near the North and South poles looks much larger than it really is. Land near the equator is more accurate in size.

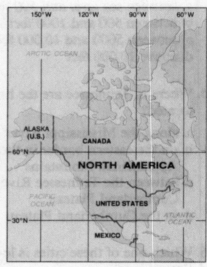

## Polar Projection

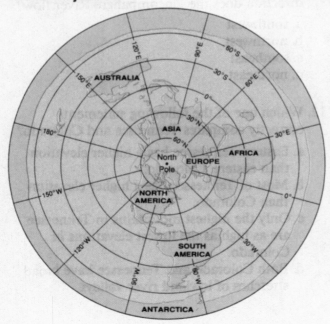

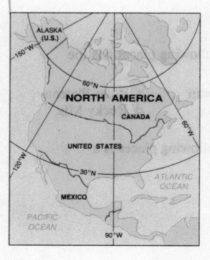

A polar projection shows Earth as if you were looking down at the North Pole or the South Pole. A polar projection often shows only half the globe.

The Mollweide Projection is called an equal-area projection. That is, land areas are accurate in size. However, shapes are distorted, especially near the edge of the map.

Study the world and North American projections shown on these pages.

## Mollweide Projection

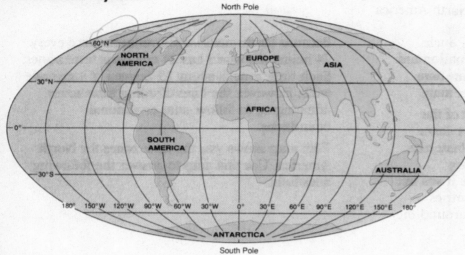

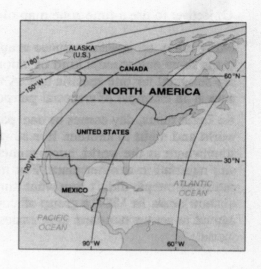

1. On which projection does Alaska look largest in comparison to other parts of the United States?

   a. polar   b. Mercator   c. Mollweide

2. On which world projection is it most difficult to see the size and shape of Mexico?

   a. polar   b. Mercator   c. Mollweide

3. Which world projection makes North America look larger than South America?

   a. polar   b. Mercator   c. Mollweide

4. On the Mollweide equal-area projection, which one of these continents looks largest?

   a. North America
   b. South America
   c. Europe
   d. Africa

5. Which world projection shows most clearly that Alaska and Russia are close to each other?

   a. polar   b. Mercator   c. Mollweide

6. Which North American map is the only projection to show curved parallels of latitude?

   a. polar   b. Mercator   c. Mollweide

7. Which world projections show most clearly that Asia lies east of Europe?

   a. polar and Mercator
   b. polar and Mollweide
   c. Mollweide and Mercator

8. Which map showing the polar projection would have the most distortion?

   a. world map
   b. North America map

9. Give one reason for your answer to question 8.

   anTart'cka Goes arona
   The woiP2

# Reading a Time Zone Map

**Objective:** to use a time zone map of North America

Many maps are **special purpose maps**. Such maps show one specific kind of information and are designed for one specific use. A **time zone map** is an example of a special purpose map.

As Earth turns, day comes to one part of the world and night to another. It is always dawn somewhere in the world, noon somewhere else, and nightfall in another place. For many centuries people didn't care what time it was in distant lands. In 1884, a group of countries agreed to set up standard time zones around the world.

Because Earth makes a full rotation once every 24 hours, the world has 24 one-hour time zones. Each time zone is about 15 degrees of longitude wide. However, the lines dividing time zones often zigzag to follow state or national boundaries.

This map shows you the time zones for North America. Use this map to answer the following questions.

**Time Zones in North America**

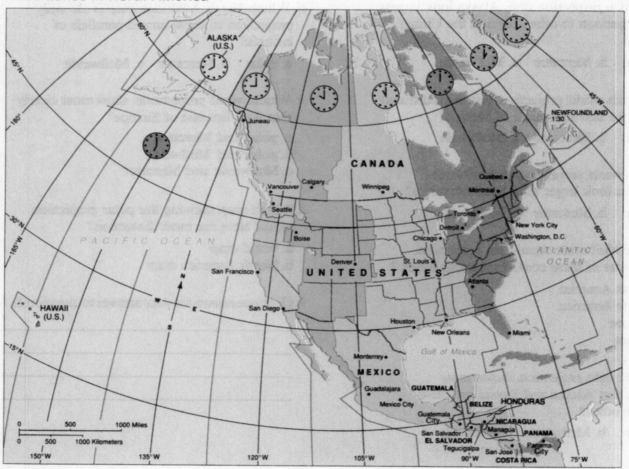

1. What time does this map show for New York City?

   a. 10:00 a.m.
   b. 12:00 noon
   c. 8:00 a.m.
   d. 6:00 p.m.

2. What time does this map show for Chicago?

   a. 1:00 p.m.
   b. 12:00 noon
   c. 11:00 a.m.
   d. 9:00 a.m.

3. What is the time difference between New York City and Chicago?

   a. It is the same time in both cities.
   b. It is an hour later in Chicago than it is in New York City.
   c. It is an hour earlier in Chicago than it is in New York City.

4. Which one of the following cities is in the same time zone as Denver?

   a. Boise
   b. Seattle
   c. Atlanta
   d. Chicago

5. Which two cities are in the same time zone as Winnipeg?

   a. Chicago and Denver
   b. Denver and Mexico City
   c. Denver and Tegucigalpa
   d. Mexico City and Tegucigalpa

6. If it is 5:00 p.m. in Washington, D.C., what time is it in San Francisco?

   a. 8:00 p.m.
   b. 2:00 p.m.
   c. 3:00 p.m.
   d. 1:00 p.m.

7. How does the time change when you cross the border from Canada into Alaska?

   a. It is two hours earlier in Alaska.
   b. It is one hour earlier in Alaska.
   c. It is two hours later in Alaska.
   d. It is one hour later in Alaska.

8. If it is 10:00 a.m. in Seattle, what time is it in St. Louis?

   a. 11:00 a.m.
   b. 8:00 a.m.
   c. 12:00 noon
   d. 2:00 p.m.

9. Suppose you are traveling by airplane from Denver east to Detroit. You leave Denver at 5:00 p.m. and the flight takes two hours. What time will you land in Detroit?

   a. 8:00 p.m.
   b. 6:00 p.m.
   c. 7:00 p.m.
   d. 9:00 p.m.

10. Suppose you are flying from New York to Juneau, Alaska. The flight takes seven hours. If you leave New York at 10:00 a.m., what time will you arrive in Juneau?

    a. 5:00 p.m.          c. 8:00 p.m.
    b. 3:00 a.m.          d. 1:00 p.m.

11. Suppose you were on a business trip that took you to many North American cities. To stay on schedule, you must set your watch ahead or back as you go from city to city and time zone to time zone. Each leg of your trip is listed below. Fill in the correct setting and number of hours for each watch change.

| | Set Watch (ahead or back?) | Number of Hours |
|---|---|---|
| a. Houston to New York | ahead | 1 |
| b. New York to Mexico City | back | 1 |
| c. Mexico City to San Francisco | back | 2 |
| d. San Francisco to Managua | ahead | 2 |
| e. Managua to Atlanta | ahead | 1 |

# Using a Highway Map

**Objectives:** to use a highway map to locate places, measure distances, and choose routes for travel

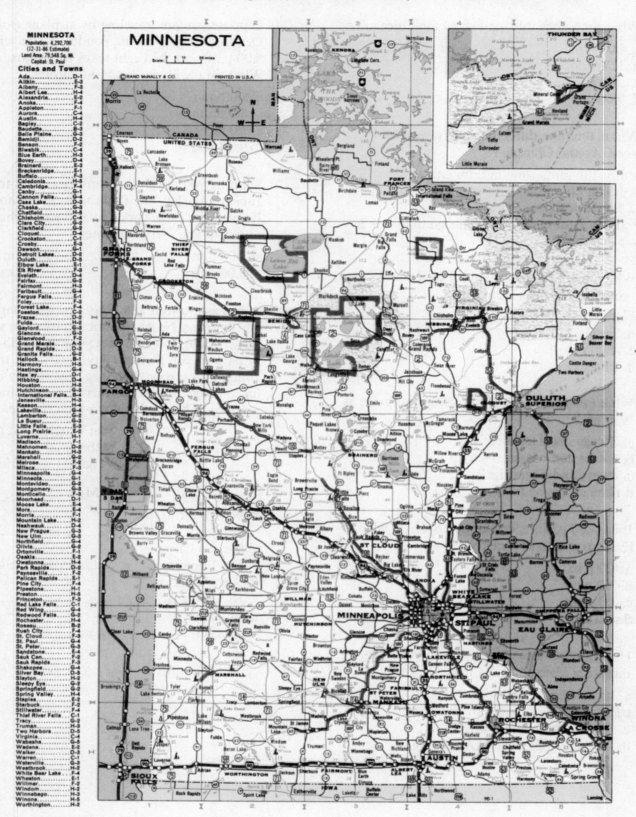

**MINNESOTA**
Population: 4,292,700
(12-31-86 Estimate)
Land Area: 79,548 Sq. Mi.
Capital: St. Paul

**Cities and Towns**

| | |
|---|---|
| Ada | D-1 |
| Aitkin | E-3 |
| Albany | F-3 |
| Albert Lea | H-4 |
| Alexandria | E-2 |
| Anoka | F-4 |
| Appleton | F-1 |
| Aurora | C-4 |
| Austin | H-4 |
| Bagley | C-2 |
| Baudette | B-3 |
| Belle Plaine | G-3 |
| Bemidji | D-2 |
| Benson | F-2 |
| Biwabik | C-4 |
| Blue Earth | H-3 |
| Bovey | D-3 |
| Brainerd | E-3 |
| Breckenridge | E-1 |
| Buffalo | F-3 |
| Caledonia | H-5 |
| Cambridge | F-4 |
| Canby | G-1 |
| Cannon Falls | G-4 |
| Cass Lake | D-3 |
| Chaska | G-3 |
| Chatfield | H-5 |
| Chisholm | C-4 |
| Clara City | G-2 |
| Clarkfield | G-2 |
| Cloquet | D-4 |
| Crookston | C-1 |
| Crosby | E-3 |
| Dawson | G-1 |
| Detroit Lakes | D-2 |
| Duluth | D-5 |
| Elbow Lake | E-1 |
| Elk River | F-3 |
| Eveleth | C-4 |
| Fairfax | G-3 |
| Fairmont | H-3 |
| Faribault | G-4 |
| Fergus Falls | E-1 |
| Foley | F-4 |
| Forest Lake | F-4 |
| Fosston | C-2 |
| Frazee | D-2 |
| Fulda | H-2 |
| Gaylord | G-3 |
| Glencoe | G-3 |
| Glenwood | F-2 |
| Grand Marais | A-5 |
| Grand Rapids | D-3 |
| Granite Falls | G-2 |
| Hallock | B-1 |
| Harmony | H-5 |
| Hastings | G-4 |
| Hawley | D-1 |
| Hibbing | D-4 |
| Houston | H-5 |
| Hutchinson | G-3 |
| International Falls | B-4 |
| Janesville | G-4 |
| Kasson | G-4 |
| Lakeville | G-4 |
| Lamberton | G-2 |
| Le Sueur | G-3 |
| Little Falls | F-3 |
| Long Prairie | E-2 |
| Luverne | H-1 |
| Madison | F-1 |
| Mahnomen | D-2 |
| Mankato | G-3 |
| Marshall | G-2 |
| Melrose | F-3 |
| Milaca | F-3 |
| Minneapolis | G-4 |
| Minnesota | G-1 |
| Montevideo | G-1 |
| Montgomery | G-3 |
| Monticello | F-3 |
| Moorhead | D-1 |
| Moose Lake | E-4 |
| Mora | F-4 |
| Morris | F-1 |
| Mountain Lake | H-2 |
| Nashwauk | C-4 |
| New Prague | G-3 |
| New Ulm | G-3 |
| Northfield | G-4 |
| Olivia | G-2 |
| Ortonville | F-1 |
| Osakis | E-2 |
| Owatonna | H-4 |
| Park Rapids | D-2 |
| Paynesville | F-2 |
| Pelican Rapids | E-1 |
| Pine City | F-4 |
| Pipestone | H-1 |
| Preston | H-5 |
| Princeton | F-3 |
| Red Lake Falls | C-1 |
| Red Wing | G-4 |
| Redwood Falls | G-2 |
| Rochester | H-4 |
| Roseau | B-2 |
| Rush City | F-4 |
| St. Cloud | F-3 |
| St. Paul | G-4 |
| St. Peter | G-3 |
| Sandstone | E-4 |
| Sauk Cen. | F-2 |
| Sauk Rapids | F-3 |
| Shakopee | G-4 |
| Silver Bay | D-5 |
| Slayton | H-2 |
| Sleepy Eye | G-2 |
| Springfield | G-2 |
| Spring Valley | H-5 |
| Staples | E-2 |
| Starbuck | F-2 |
| Stillwater | F-4 |
| Thief River Falls | C-1 |
| Tracy | G-2 |
| Truman | H-3 |
| Two Harbors | D-5 |
| Virginia | C-4 |
| Wabasha | G-5 |
| Wadena | E-2 |
| Walker | D-3 |
| Warren | B-1 |
| Waterville | G-4 |
| Westhook | H-2 |
| White Bear Lake | F-4 |
| Wheaton | E-1 |
| Willmar | F-2 |
| Windom | H-2 |
| Winnebago | H-3 |
| Winona | H-5 |
| Worthington | H-2 |

A **highway map** is useful when you are traveling. Its letter-number index helps you locate cities and towns. The small square inset map at the upper right shows the rest of northeastern Minnesota. You can use the map scale to find distances between places.

Use the highway map of Minnesota on the previous page to answer the following questions.

1. What is the location of Duluth?

    a. D-5
    b. E-4
    c. E-5
    d. D-3

2. What interstate highway connects Duluth with Minneapolis?

    a. Interstate 90
    b. Interstate 35
    c. Interstate 94
    d. Interstate 29

3. What highway would you take from Duluth to travel along the northern shore of Lake Superior?

    a. State Route 13
    b. Interstate 35
    c. U.S. Route 61
    d. U.S. Route 53

4. What state borders Minnesota on the south?

    a. Wisconsin
    b. South Dakota
    c. Iowa
    d. Michigan

5. Find Fergus Falls. What direction would you travel to go from Minneapolis to Fergus Falls?

    a. south
    b. north
    c. southeast
    d. northwest

6. How far is Fargo from Minneapolis if you travel on Interstate 94?

    a. about 250 mi
    b. about 180 mi
    c. about 210 mi
    d. about 150 mi

7. What route would you travel from Austin to Sioux Falls?

    a. Interstate 35
    b. U.S. Route 69
    c. Interstate 90
    d. U.S. Route 14

8. About how far is Sioux Falls from Austin?

    a. about 170 mi
    b. about 120 mi
    c. about 200 mi
    d. about 230 mi

9. The red numbers along highways indicate distances between the places. On Interstate 90, what is the distance between Blue Earth and Jackson?

    a. about 15 mi
    b. about 45 mi
    c. about 28 mi
    d. about 20 mi

10. What is the distance from International Falls to Baudette along State Route 11?

    a. about 71 mi
    b. about 33 mi
    c. about 59 mi
    d. about 11 mi

11. If you traveled from Brainerd (E-3) to Detroit Lakes (D-2) along highway 10, through which of these cities would you pass?

    a. Motley and Pequot Lakes
    b. Motley and New York Mills
    c. New York Mills and Sebeka
    d. Motley and Sebeka

12. What is the shortest route from Minneapolis to Blue Earth?

    a. Go southeast on U.S. Route 52 to Rochester. Turn west on Interstate 90.
    b. Go south on Interstate 35 to Interstate 90. Turn west on Interstate 90.
    c. Go southwest on U.S. Route 169 to State Route 60. Take Route 60 southwest to Interstate 90. Turn east on Interstate 90.

# Using a City Map

**Objectives:** to apply map-reading skills to a city map

A map can help you locate places in an unfamiliar city. This map shows the city of Phoenix, Arizona. Suppose that you have just arrived at the Phoenix Sky Harbor International Airport. You rent a car to travel around the city. Use the map to answer the following questions.

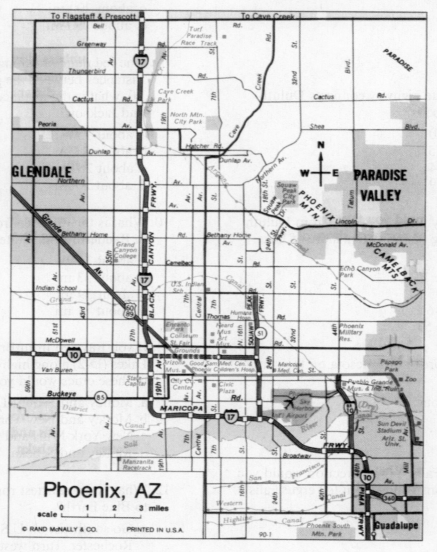

1. Which phrase best describes the location of Phoenix Sky Harbor International Airport?

   a. north of Cactus Rd. and west of Scottsdale Rd.

   b. east of Grand Ave. and west of Interstate 17

   c. east of 24th St. and south of Van Buren St.

   d. north of McDowell Rd. and south of Indian School Rd.

2. Suppose you wanted to begin your trip by visiting the state capitol. Where is it located?

   a. 19th Ave.

   b. University Dr.

   c. Thomas Rd.

   d. 16th St.

3. What direction would you go from the airport to reach the capitol?

   a. east
   b. west
   c. north
   d. south

4. Which one of the following routes would you take to reach the state capitol?

   a. south on 40th St. and east on Broadway
   b. west on Buckeye Rd. and north on 19th Ave.
   c. north on 40th St. and east on Van Buren St.

5. Which one of the following places is closest to the state capitol?

   a. Grand Canyon College
   b. Maricopa Medical Center
   c. Civic Plaza
   d. Arizona Museum

6. How many canals does the Black Canyon Freeway cross?

   a. 1           c. 4
   b. 2           d. 5

7. About how far is it from the zoo to Arizona State University?

   a. 2.5 mi      c. 1.5 mi
   b. 4 mi        d. 6 mi

8. Which one of these is generally located north of Camelback Rd. and west of 43rd Ave.?

   a. Camelback Mts.
   b. Paradise Valley
   c. Glendale
   d. Salt River

9. If you were traveling by car following the most direct route, which of these would be the greatest distance to travel?

   a. from Maricopa Medical Center to the U.S. Indian School
   b. from the U.S. Indian School to the Black Canyon Freeway
   c. from the state capitol to the Maricopa Freeway
   d. from Grand Canyon College to the Maricopa Medical Center

Tourists visit the Phoenix Civic Plaza on Central Avenue

10. You have left Squaw Peak City Park and are ready to turn onto Lincoln Dr. What is the shortest route from there to Guadalupe?

    a. Go east on Lincoln Dr. to Tatum Blvd. Go north on Tatum Blvd. about 5 mi.
    b. Go east on Lincoln Dr. to 24th St. Go south on 24th St. to the Maricopa Freeway. Go east on the freeway for about 8 mi.
    c. Go west on Lincoln Dr. to Central Ave. Go south on Central Ave. to Broadway. Go west on Broadway for about 8 mi.

11. Follow these directions on the map. Start in Paradise Valley. Go west on Lincoln Dr. to the Black Canyon Freeway. Go north on the freeway until you come to the first street past Thunderbird Rd. Go east on that road for about 3 miles. Where are you?

    a. North Mt. City Park
    b. Encanto Park Coliseum
    c. Glendale
    d. Turf Paradise Race Track

12. Explain how to get from Grand Canyon College to the Sun Devil Stadium. Include compass directions and distances in your answer.

    _____
    _____
    _____
    _____
    _____
    _____

# Reading an Historical Map

**Objectives:** to interpret an historical map and draw conclusions from the information

An historical map is a type of special purpose map. **Historical maps** show many different kinds of information about the past.

This map shows the thirteen original states of the United States. It also shows lands they claimed outside the borders they have today. These land claims date back to the 1600s and early 1700s, when European settlers knew little about the inland parts of North America.

After the United States won its independence, the states gave up, or ceded, their land claims. Most of the land was ceded to the federal government to form new states. Sometimes, however, one state ceded land to another state with a better claim.

Use the map to answer the following questions.

**Lands Claimed by Original States**

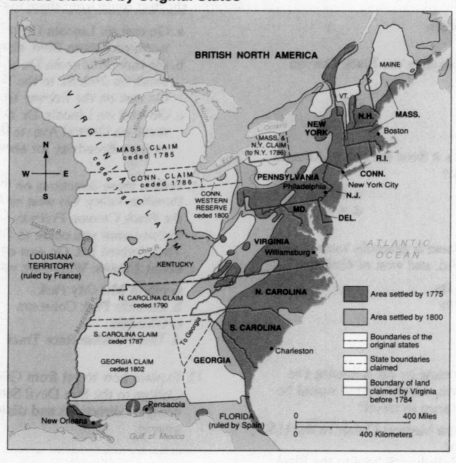

1. Where did most of the early settlement in the thirteen original states take place?

   a. along the coast of the Gulf of Mexico
   b. along the Mississippi River
   c. around the Great Lakes
   d. along the coast of the Atlantic Ocean

2. Generally in what direction did European settlers move to settle new areas?

   a. south
   b. north
   c. east
   d. west

3. Before 1784, what state had claimed the largest area of land?

   a. New York
   b. Virginia
   c. North Carolina
   d. Pennsylvania

4. In 1800, what was the westernmost boundary of the lands claimed by the states?

   a. Atlantic Ocean
   b. Gulf of Mexico
   c. Mississippi River
   d. Great Lakes

5. In 1800, what state governed the area that is now the state of Maine?

   a. Massachusetts
   b. Virginia
   c. New York
   d. New Hampshire

6. Which one of these states claimed no western lands?

   a. Connecticut      c. New Jersey
   b. Georgia          d. North Carolina

7. About how wide, from east to west, would North Carolina's northern border have been if it had kept all land it claimed before 1790?

   a. 225 mi           c. 780 mi
   b. 90 mi            d. 550 mi

8. In what year did Massachusetts give up its land claim along Lake Erie and Lake Ontario?

   a. 1786   b. 1800   c. 1785   d. 1792

9. About how many miles is it from Philadelphia to New York City?

   a. 50 mi            c. 200 mi
   b. 150 mi           d. 100 mi

10. What was the largest area to be settled between 1775 and 1800?

    a. the area claimed by Connecticut
    b. the area that became the state of Kentucky
    c. the areas along the Mississippi and Missouri rivers
    d. the area around the Great Lakes

11. Which one of the following places was outside United States' territory in 1800?

    a. New Orleans
    b. Kentucky
    c. Lake Michigan
    d. Delaware

12. How did most early settlers probably reach New Orleans?

    a. They traveled overland from eastern states such as Georgia.
    b. They traveled south along rivers from states such as Kentucky.
    c. They traveled east by boat across the Gulf of Mexico.
    d. They traveled east overland from beyond the Mississippi River.

13. Which generalization about the states' western claims is correct?

    a. States claimed only lands that were directly west of their own boundaries.
    b. States that had other states on their western borders made no claims in the western lands.
    c. Western lands were often claimed by more than one state.

14. Suppose it is 1800 and you want to build a trading post in an expanding, growing area of the United States. What would be the best place to build your fort?

    a. near New York City
    b. in eastern South Carolina, near the Atlantic coast
    c. near where the Mississippi River joins the Ohio River
    d. on the southern shore of Lake Erie

15. Give one reason for your answer to question 14.

    _____
    _____
    _____
    _____

# Comparing Historical Maps

**Objective:** to identify historical changes by comparing maps

In 1776, the United States was a narrow strip of land along the Atlantic coast. By 1853, the nation stretched from the Atlantic to the Pacific.

The maps on this page show how the territory of the United States grew.

### U.S. 13 COLONIES—1776

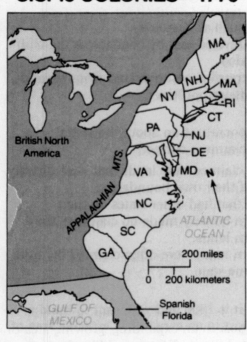

### UNITED STATES—1803

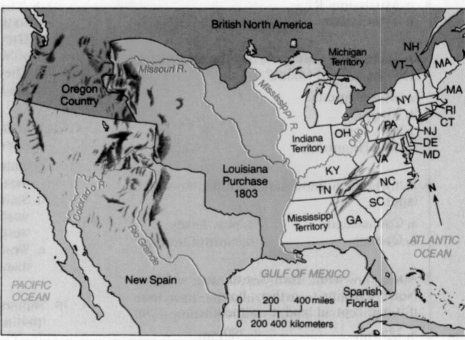

### UNITED STATES—1783

### UNITED STATES—1803-1853

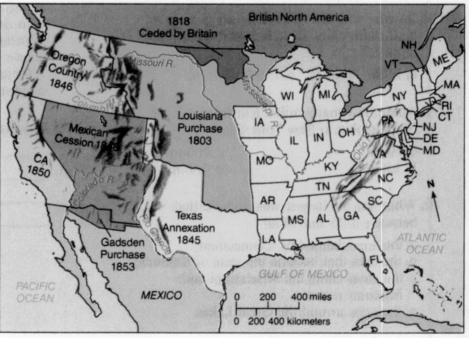

Use the maps to answer the following questions.

1. What natural feature formed the western frontier of the 13 original colonies?

    a. Mississippi River
    b. Appalachian Mts.
    c. Rocky Mts.
    d. Pacific Ocean

2. What country held the land west of the 13 original colonies before 1783?

    a. Great Britain
    b. Spain
    c. France
    d. Mexico

3. What natural feature became the western border of the United States according to the Treaty of Paris in 1783?

    a. Mississippi River
    b. Appalachian Mts.
    c. Rocky Mts.
    d. Pacific Ocean

4. What country kept control of most of the land north of the United States from 1776-1853?

    a. France
    b. Spain
    c. Great Britain
    d. Russia

5. In what year did the United States make the Louisiana Purchase?

    a. 1783   b. 1800   c. 1753   d. 1803

6. Which one of the following states was not one of the 13 original colonies but was a state by the time of the Louisiana Purchase?

    a. New Hampshire
    b. Massachusetts
    c. Rhode Island
    d. Vermont

7. What was the last area east of the Mississippi River to become part of the United States?

    a. Maine
    b. Texas
    c. Florida
    d. Georgia

8. What country controlled most of the land west of the Louisiana Purchase in 1803?

    a. United States
    b. Spain
    c. France
    d. Mexico

9. Which statement about the westward expansion of the United States between 1776 and 1803 is true?

    a. Each time the nation expanded, it at least doubled in size.
    b. The United States added only lands that its citizens had already settled.
    c. The nation expanded little by little, adding small amounts of territory.
    d. In general, the United States was uninterested in expanding to the west.

10. After the Louisiana Purchase, which one of these was the next western land the United States gained?

    a. Oregon
    b. Texas
    c. Mexican Cession
    d. Gadsden Purchase

11. In what year did the United States first gain territory on the Pacific Coast?

    a. 1803   b. 1846   c. 1848   d. 1819

12. What territory did the United States gain from Great Britain?

    a. Florida
    b. Gadsden Purchase
    c. Texas
    d. Oregon

13. During which decade did the United States gain the most land?

    a. 1810-1820
    b. 1840-1850
    c. 1780-1790
    d. 1800-1810

14. By 1853, which one of the following rivers formed a boundary between the United States and another country?

    a. Mississippi
    b. Missouri
    c. Columbia
    d. Rio Grande

15. What can you infer about the possession of land in North America?

    a. The United States gained land by agreements, purchases, wars, and treaties.
    b. Except for the United States, few countries were interested in lands on the North American continent.
    c. Nothing could have prevented the United States from expanding to the Pacific, because the Pacific is the only natural boundary for the country.

# Reading a Climate Map

**Objective:** to use a climate map to describe and compare the climates of various locations

**Climate** is the weather pattern in a region over many years. One important part of climate is **temperature**. A second important part of climate is **precipitation**, or moisture. Precipitation includes both rain and snow.

This map shows the climate regions across the United States. Use the map to answer the following questions.

## U.S. CLIMATE REGIONS

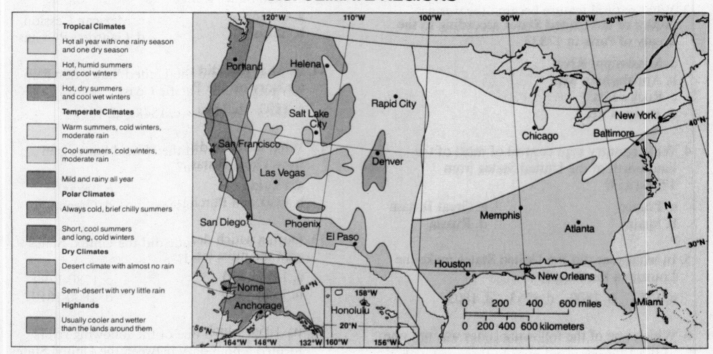

1. Which one of the following cities has a climate that is hot or warm all year?

   a. Denver
   b. Miami
   c. Honolulu
   d. Baltimore

2. What kind of climate does Chicago, Illinois, probably have?

   a. desert climate with almost no rain
   b. mild and rainy all year
   c. warm, rainy summers and cold winters
   d. short summers and long, cold, snowy winters

3. Which one of the following cities has a climate that is semi-desert with very little rain?

   a. New Orleans
   b. Helena
   c. Chicago
   d. Honolulu

4. Which of these cities probably records the lowest temperatures?

   a. Las Vegas
   b. Anchorage
   c. Helena
   d. Nome

5. Which one of the following cities probably has a climate most like El Paso, Texas?

   a. Houston
   b. Memphis
   c. Las Vegas
   d. San Diego

6. Which city probably gets the most rain?

   a. Portland
   b. Salt Lake City
   c. New Orleans
   d. Anchorage

7. Which one of the following cities probably gets the least rain?

   a. San Francisco
   b. New Orleans
   c. New York City
   d. Phoenix

8. What kind of climate covers most of the United States east of 90° W longitude?

   a. cool summers, cold winters
   b. mild and rainy all year
   c. desert with almost no rain
   d. hot, humid summers and cool winters

9. Which one of the following statements is characteristic of temperate climates?

   a. always cold, brief chilly summers
   b. semi-desert with very little rain
   c. mild and rainy all year
   d. hot all year with one rainy season and one dry season

10. Find the approximate location of your city on the map. What kind of climate does it have?

   _____

11. Write a few sentences describing the climate of the Hawaiian Islands.

   _____

   _____

   _____

   _____

12. What conclusion can be drawn about the relationship between climate and latitude?

   _____

   _____

   _____

   _____

13. Based on this map, where would you expect to find a mountain range in the United States?

   a. extending east and west along the border with Canada
   b. stretching north and south in the western half of the United States
   c. curving along the eastern coast from New York to Miami
   d. running east and west across the center of the country from San Francisco to Chicago

Saguaro, the largest cactus in the U.S., grows in the deserts of Arizona and California.

# Reading a Weather Map

**Objectives:** to gather information, interpret symbols, and draw conclusions from a weather map

A **weather map** is a special purpose map that you see every day in the newspaper or on the television weather forecast. Remember winds are named for the direction they blow <u>from</u>.

Therefore, a south wind is blowing <u>from</u> the south <u>toward</u> the north. Also, most weather systems move from west to east.

This map shows a day's weather conditions in the United States.

## WEATHER MAP

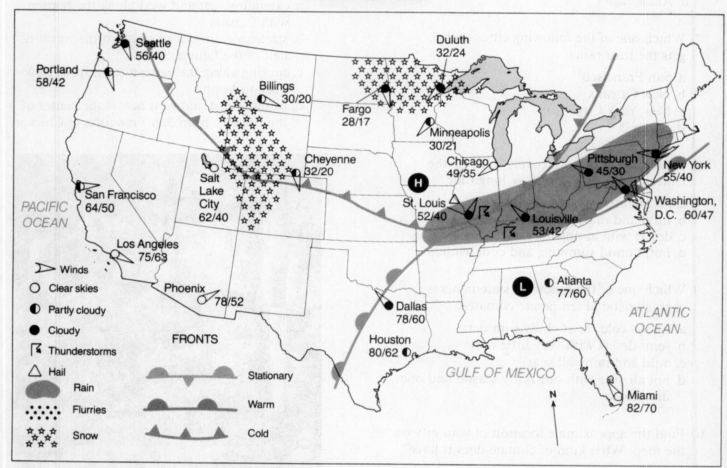

1. Which statement best describes the weather in San Francisco for the day shown on the map?

   a. It will be cloudy with a high of 64°F and a low of 50°F.
   b. It will be clear with a high of 42°F and a low of 32°F.
   c. It will be partly cloudy with a high of 64°F and a low of 50°F.
   d. It will be partly cloudy with a high of 42°F and a low of 32°F.

2. Which statement best describes the weather in Pittsburgh?

   a. It will be clear with a northwest wind and a high of 45°F.
   b. It will be cloudy with a southeast wind and a high of 30°F.
   c. It will be rainy with a northwest wind and a high of 45°F.
   d. It will be rainy with a southeast wind and a high of 30°F.

3. Which one of the following cities is predicted to have thunderstorms with hail?

   a. Louisville
   b. St. Louis
   c. Duluth
   d. Cheyenne

4. What kind of front stretches from Seattle to east of the Great Lakes?

   a. cold front
   b. warm front
   c. stationary front

5. Which one of the following cities is expected to have snow?

   a. Seattle
   b. New York City
   c. Fargo
   d. Portland

6. How would a weather forecaster describe the wind in Cheyenne, Wyoming?

   a. east wind
   b. west wind
   c. south wind
   d. north wind

7. Based on the information on this map, where are thunderstorms most likely to occur?

   a. in a high pressure system
   b. in a low pressure system
   c. where a cold front and a warm front meet
   d. where snow is falling

8. In what city do a cold and warm front almost meet?

   _____

9. If you were traveling from Salt Lake City to Cheyenne, what kind of weather would you probably be driving in?

   _____

10. If you lived in Louisville, how would you dress for the weather on this particular day?

    _____

    _____

11. Which city has had a cold front move south of it, lies between areas of rain and snow, but expects partly cloudly skies and a high temperature of 30° F?

    a. Billings        c. New York
    b. Minneapolis     d. Fargo

12. Choose one city shown on the map and write a weather forecast for it on the lines below.

    _____

    _____

    _____

    _____

    _____

    _____

    _____

# Reading Special Purpose Maps

**Objectives:** to gather information, make comparisons, and draw conclusions
from special purpose maps

A special purpose map gives specific information
about an area.

The maps on these pages show precipitation and
vegetation in the United States. Because the type

of vegetation that grows in an area depends on
rainfall, these two maps are often compared.
Use both of these maps to answer the following
questions.

## U.S. PRECIPITATION

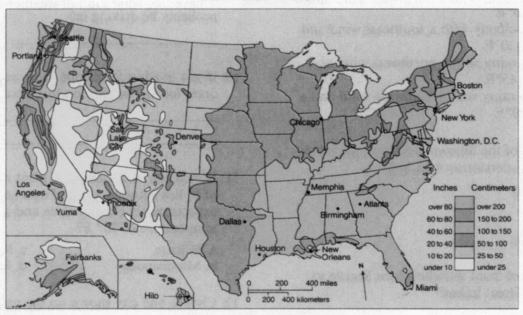

## U.S. NATURAL VEGETATION

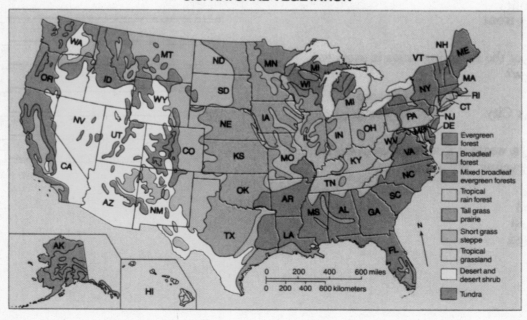

1. Which one of the following regions has the heaviest annual rainfall?

   a. the northwestern coastal region
   b. the midwestern plains
   c. the southeastern coastal region
   d. the northern central lakes region

2. In general, which section of the United States has the least rainfall?

   a. northwest            c. southeast
   b. northeast            d. southwest

3. Which one of the following states gets the most rain in an average year?

   a. Ohio
   b. Hawaii
   c. New York
   d. Minnesota

4. What is the average annual rainfall in Arkansas?

   a. between 20 and 40 inches
   b. 40 inches
   c. 60 inches
   d. between 40 and 60 inches

5. What type of vegetation grows naturally in the state of Georgia?

   a. tall grass prairie
   b. desert and desert shrub
   c. mixed broadleaf and evergreen forest
   d. tundra

6. Which one of the following states has mainly desert and desert shrub vegetation?

   a. Kansas               c. Texas
   b. Nevada               d. Florida

7. Where in the United States are the largest areas of tundra?

   a. Colorado             c. Alaska
   b. Oregon               d. California

8. What is the most widespread vegetation in parts of the country that get more than 40 inches of rain a year?

   a. woodland and shrub
   b. mixed tall grass and short grass
   c. tundra and alpine vegetation
   d. mixed broadleaf and evergreen forest

9. How much rainfall do most grasslands get each year?

   a. 60 to 80 in.         c. 10 to 20 in.
   b. 10 to 40 in.         d. 20 to 60 in.

10. What is the least rainfall that seems to allow forests to grow?

   a. 60 in.               c. 20 in.
   b. 10 in.               d. 80 in.

11. What kind of vegetation do you find in places with less than 10 inches of rain a year?

   a. short grass steppe
   b. tundra
   c. evergreen forest
   d. desert and desert shrub

12. What is the most common rainfall in the mixed evergreen and broadleaf forests along the eastern coast of the United States?

   a. 20 to 40 in.         c. 10 to 20 in.
   b. 40 to 60 in.         d. 60 to 80 in.

13. What kind of vegetation is most common in the region east of Colorado, where the rainfall is 10 to 40 inches a year?

   a. evergreen and broadleaf forests
   b. desert and desert shrub
   c. short grass steppe
   d. tall grass prairie

14. Suppose you wanted to vacation in a state with the greatest variety of vegetation. Which one of the following states would you choose?

   a. Kansas               c. California
   b. Alaska               d. Hawaii

# Comparing Special Purpose Maps

**Objectives:** to gather information, make comparisons, and draw conclusions
about topography and land using special purpose maps

**Topography** is the description of the surface of
land. A topographical map gives you information
about elevation and relief. **Relief** describes how
rugged or flat land is. Rugged lands, such as
mountains, have high relief. Level lands, such as
plains, have low relief.

A **land-use map** shows how people use the soil,
vegetation, and mineral resources of an area.

These maps show topography and land use in the
state of New York. Use the maps to answer the
following questions.

## TOPOGRAPHY OF NEW YORK

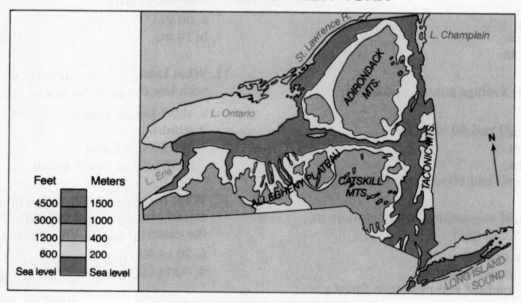

## LAND USE IN NEW YORK

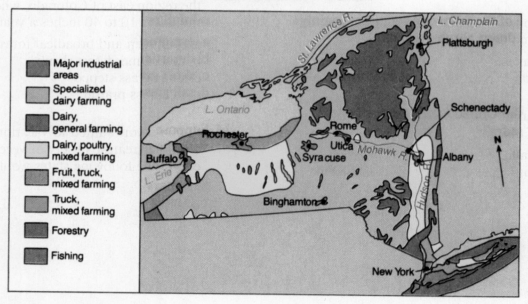

1. Which one of these regions in New York has the highest relief?

   a. Adirondack Mts.
   b. Hudson River valley
   c. Allegheny Plateau
   d. Long Island

2. Which one of these regions has the lowest elevation?

   a. Allegheny Plateau
   b. Catskill Mts.
   c. Long Island
   d. Adirondack Mts.

3. What type of land use covers the largest area in New York?

   a. major industrial areas
   b. forests
   c. fruit, truck, and mixed farming
   d. specialized dairy farming

4. Which one of the following items is an important product between sea level and 600 feet along the shore of Lake Ontario?

   a. fruit
   b. fish
   c. cattle
   d. poultry

5. What is the elevation of the largest forest regions?

   a. between 3000 and 4500 feet
   b. between 1200 feet and 3000 feet
   c. between sea level and 600 feet
   d. between 600 and 1200 feet

6. What is the elevation of most of the major dairy regions?

   a. between sea level and 600 feet
   b. between 3000 and 4500 feet
   c. between 600 and 1200 feet
   d. between 1200 and 3000 feet

7. If you lived in the area of the Allegheny Plateau, what two products might your farm produce?

   a. fruit and trees
   b. fruit and dairy products
   c. dairy products and poultry
   d. poultry and trees

8. Which one of these cities is located near an important forestry area?

   a. Binghamton
   b. Rochester
   c. Buffalo
   d. Plattsburgh

9. Which one of these cities is a major industrial area near truck farming?

   a. New York City
   b. Buffalo
   c. Albany
   d. Schenectady

10. What do all the industrial areas in New York have in common?

    a. They are all in the northern part of the state.
    b. They are all located along waterways.
    c. They are all surrounded by dairy farms.
    d. They are all located near large deposits of iron ore.

11. What statement best describes the topography of New York State?

    a. Rugged mountains over 4500 feet high cover most of the state.
    b. Lands below sea level cover most of the state, with high mountains along Lake Ontario.
    c. Lands of 1200 to 3000 feet cover most of the state with low mountains along Long Island Sound.
    d. A mixture of lowlands, low mountains and hills cover the state.

12. Which area of New York would be most affected by an extremely rainy spring that flooded low croplands and polluted fishing waters with toxic run-off?

    a. around New York City and Long Island Sound
    b. along the St. Lawrence River and Lake Champlain
    c. through central New York from Rome to Binghamton
    d. in the Adirondack Mts. near Plattsburgh

# Interpreting an Historical Map

**Objectives:** to gather information and draw conclusions from a map of an historic battle

An historical map can sometimes help you understand or experience a past event. The Battle of Gettysburg in 1863 was the turning point in the Civil War. The map below shows troop positions and the lay of the land around Gettysburg, Pennsylvania. The short lines drawn close together indicate hills. In the three-day

battle that followed, Confederate troops repeatedly attacked Union lines. The Union army held its ground, however. With heavy losses, Lee finally retreated. Together, the two sides lost 51,000 men killed, wounded, or missing.

## BATTLE OF GETTYSBURG, JULY 2, 1863

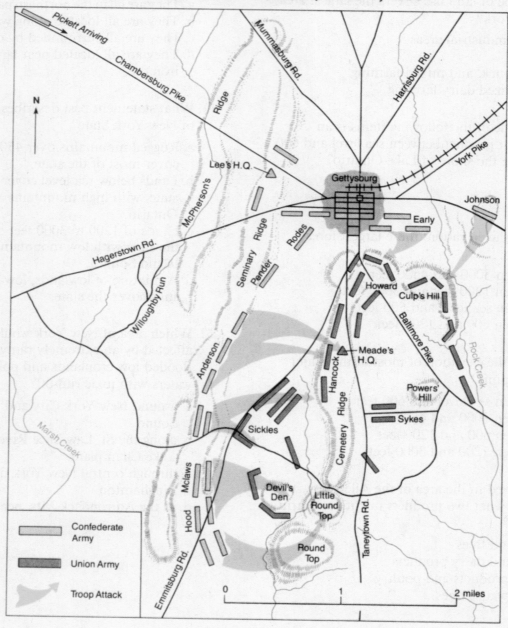

1. Where did most of the fighting take place, in relation to the town of Gettysburg?

   a. south of the town
   b. north of the town
   c. west of the town
   d. east of the town

2. Which one of the following areas was held by the Confederate army?

   a. Culp's Hill
   b. Cemetery Ridge
   c. Seminary Ridge
   d. Powers' Hill

3. Which one of the following areas was held by the Union army?

   a. Seminary Ridge
   b. Cemetery Ridge
   c. McPherson's Ridge
   d. Willoughby Run

4. How far apart were Lee's headquarters and Meade's headquarters?

   a. about 10 mi
   b. about 5 mi
   c. about 1¾ mi
   d. about 3 mi

5. Who attacked Culp's Hill?

   a. Union troops under General Slocum
   b. Confederate troops under General Johnson
   c. Union troops under General Johnson
   d. Confederate troops under General Slocum

6. What area was captured by Confederate troops under McLaws?

   a. Little Round Top
   b. Devil's Den
   c. Lee's H.Q.
   d. Cemetery Ridge

7. By what route was Pickett's division arriving?

   a. Chambersburg Pike
   b. Emmitsburg Rd.
   c. Baltimore Pike
   d. Taneytown Rd.

8. What Union general commanded troops stationed southwest of Powers' Hill?

   a. McLaws         c. Sykes
   b. Hancock      d. Hood

9. Based on information on the map, what problem did the Confederate army face in the battle?

   a. The Confederate army was trapped against a river.
   b. Confederate troops had to advance uphill to attack the Union army.
   c. Confederate troops were vastly outnumbered.
   d. The Confederate army was surrounded by Union troops.

10. Which one of the following routes did General Lee probably choose for his army's retreat?

   a. Baltimore Pike     c. Taneytown Rd.
   b. Hagerstown Rd.   d. Harrisburg Rd.

11. Give two reasons why you chose your answer to question 10.

   _____

   _____

   _____

   _____

   _____

   _____

Memorial stands today in Gettysburg, marking site of the great Civil War battle.

# Analyzing Map Data

**Objective:** to analyze advantages and disadvantages of several locations to solve a problem

A city's location is the key to its growth and success. The letters on this map show possible locations for a new city.

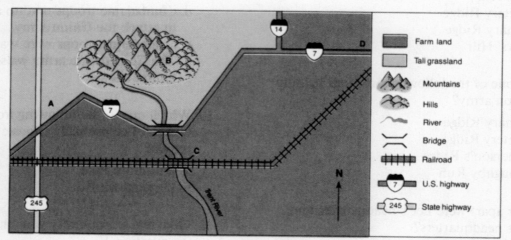

1. Which point would be the best location for a city?

   a. A  b. B  c. C  d. D

2. On the lines below, write one reason for the answer you chose.

   _____

   _____

3. What is a major disadvantage of point B as a location for a city?

   a. It is too far from transportation routes.
   b. It is too far from the mining areas in the mountains.
   c. It is too close to the large farms.
   d. It is too close to the river, which may flood.

4. What is an advantage of point C for a city?

   a. It is in the heart of the mountains, where valuable minerals are mined.
   b. It is near a major north-south highway.
   c. It is near a major U.S. highway, a railroad, and a river.
   d. It is near the intersection of two main highways.

5. What is an advantage of point D for a city?

   a. It is on a river that can be used for shipping.
   b. It is near a major source of lumber.
   c. It is at the intersection of two main highways.
   d. It is on a main highway near a railroad line.

6. What is an advantage of point A for a city?

   a. It is on a main highway and a railroad.
   b. It is near the intersection of two highways.
   c. It is on a river that can be used for shipping.
   d. It is located at sea level.

7. What is a possible disadvantage of point A?

   a. It is not near a major U. S. highway.
   b. It is not near any farming regions.
   c. It is not on a railroad line.
   d. It is not in an area with available land for growth.

8. How could point A be improved for a city?

   a. Close Highway 7 and build an interstate highway south of the railroad.
   b. Build a connecting railroad line northward from the main line, running east of Highway 245.
   c. Dam the river south of the highway bridge.

# Finding the Best Location

**Objective:** to analyze several locations according to given criteria to solve a problem

A good port city must be located on an ocean or a major waterway, be near a sheltered body of water and have an overland transportation network. The letters on this map show possible locations for a new port.

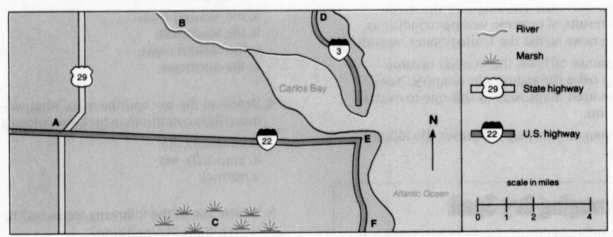

1. Which point would be the best location for a port?

   a. D   b. F   c. E   d. B

2. On the lines below, write one reason for the answer you chose.

   _____

   _____

   _____

3. What is one major disadvantage of point D as a port city?

   a. It lacks a sheltered body of water such as a bay or a cove, which an irregular coastline provides.
   b. It is too far from the ocean to take advantage of international shipping lanes.
   c. It is too far from a highway to exchange goods with inland areas.
   d. It is in a marshy area where construction would be difficult.

4. About how wide is Carlos Bay at its mouth?

   a. 3 miles          c. 0.5 miles
   b. 1.5 miles        d. 4 miles

5. What direction would you travel to go from point D to point A?

   a. southeast          c. northeast
   b. northwest          d. southwest

6. What is a major advantage of point B as a port?

   a. It is located at the intersection of two main highways.
   b. It is located on the coastline of the ocean.
   c. It is located south of Carlos Bay.
   d. It is located on a sheltered waterway connected to the ocean.

7. What location meets <u>none</u> of the criteria for a good port?

   a. F   b. C   c. A   d. E

8. How could point B be improved as a port?

   a. Cut a canal from point B to point D to link B to the ocean.
   b. Drain the marshlands surrounding point B.
   c. Build a highway from Route 29 to Route 3 with a bridge at point B.
   d. Fill in the narrow, northwestern end of Carlos Bay to give the city at point B more room to expand.

# Analyzing Current Events Maps

**Objectives:** to gather information from maps about current events and to draw conclusions and make generalizations or inferences based on map data

Newspapers, news magazines, and television news programs frequently use maps to help explain news events. The maps in this lesson show the results of extreme weather conditions that made news across the United States recently.

In the summer of 1988, the weather became front-page news throughout the country. News magazines used maps such as this one to explain the situation.

Use the map on this page to answer the following questions.

## A Damaging Dry Spell

More than 20 states have declared drought emergencies.

Drought conditions
- Extreme
- Severe
- Moderate
- Moist

SOURCE: NATIONAL OCEANIC AND
ATMOSPHERIC ADMINISTRATION;
THE DEPARTMENT OF AGRICULTURE
IB OHLSSON-NEWSWEEK

1. What is the topic that is presented by this map?

   a. the effects of extremely cold weather
   b. the effects of extremely dry weather
   c. the effects of normal summer weather
   d. the effects of erosion in farming areas

2. Which region of the United States was hardest hit by the drought?

   a. the northeast
   b. the southeast
   c. the northern midwest
   d. the southern midwest

3. What part of the country had moist conditions?

   a. the western coast
   b. the southwest
   c. the eastern coast
   d. the northeast

4. Based on the key and the map, what were the most likely conditions in the areas colored gray?

   a. unusually dry
   b. unusually wet
   c. normal

5. Which one of the following states had the widest range of conditions?

   a. Idaho
   b. Texas
   c. Florida
   d. Missouri

6. Farmers in the northern midwest depend on rain for their corn and soybean crops. What effect did weather conditions there probably have on those crops?

   a. Crop output was much lower than normal.
   b. Crop output was much higher than normal.
   c. Crop output was very close to normal.

7. Locate your state on the map. What were the weather conditions like there during the summer months of 1988?

   _____

   _____

   _____

   _____

   _____

   _____

This combined map shows another result of unusual weather conditions. The large map shows part of the state of Utah. The small one shows the whole state of Utah and part of neighboring states. A red box on the small map helps you locate the area covered by the large map. Small maps such as this one are called **insets**.

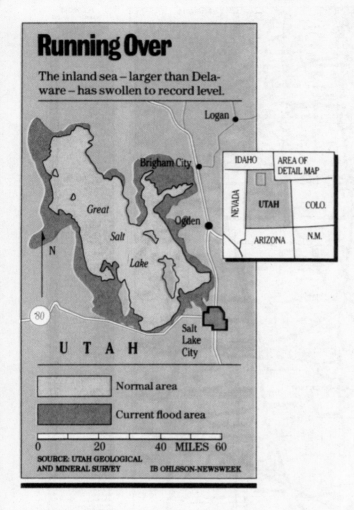

**Running Over**

The inland sea – larger than Delaware – has swollen to record level.

Logan

Brigham City

Great

Salt

Ogden

N

Lake

80

Salt Lake City

U T A H

Normal area

Current flood area

0    20    40  MILES  60

SOURCE: UTAH GEOLOGICAL
AND MINERAL SURVEY    IB OHLSSON-NEWSWEEK

AREA OF DETAIL MAP

IDAHO

NEVADA

UTAH    COLO.

ARIZONA    N.M.

8. What situation does this map show?

a. A drought in Utah led to the shrinking of the Great Salt Lake.
b. High rainfall and melting snow enlarged the Great Salt Lake.
c. The water level of the Great Salt Lake was about normal.

9. In what part of Utah is the Great Salt Lake located?

a. northern
b. southern
c. southeastern
d. central

10. How far is it from Brigham City to Ogden?

a. about 20 mi
b. about 50 mi
c. about 100 mi
d. about 70 mi

11. What is the largest city shown on this map?

a. Ogden
b. Salt Lake City
c. Brigham City
d. Logan

12. What state lies southeast of Utah?

a. Colorado
b. Nevada
c. Arizona
d. New Mexico

13. Which pair of cities was most threatened with flooding?

a. Logan and Ogden
b. Brigham City and Ogden
c. Brigham City and Salt Lake City
d. Logan and Salt Lake City

14. Which statement about Interstate 80 was probably true?

a. The highway was not affected by the rising water and remained open to traffic.
b. The highway was sometimes closed because of flooding west of Salt Lake City.
c. The highway was sometimes closed because of flooding east of Salt Lake City.

15. Which statement best describes the changes in the Great Salt Lake?

a. The lake grew to nearly three times its normal size.
b. The lake shrank to about half its normal size.
c. The lake decreased to about one third its normal size.
d. The lake increased to nearly twice its normal size.

# Finding the Best Route

**Objectives:** to locate places, measure distances, and evaluate routes on a highway map

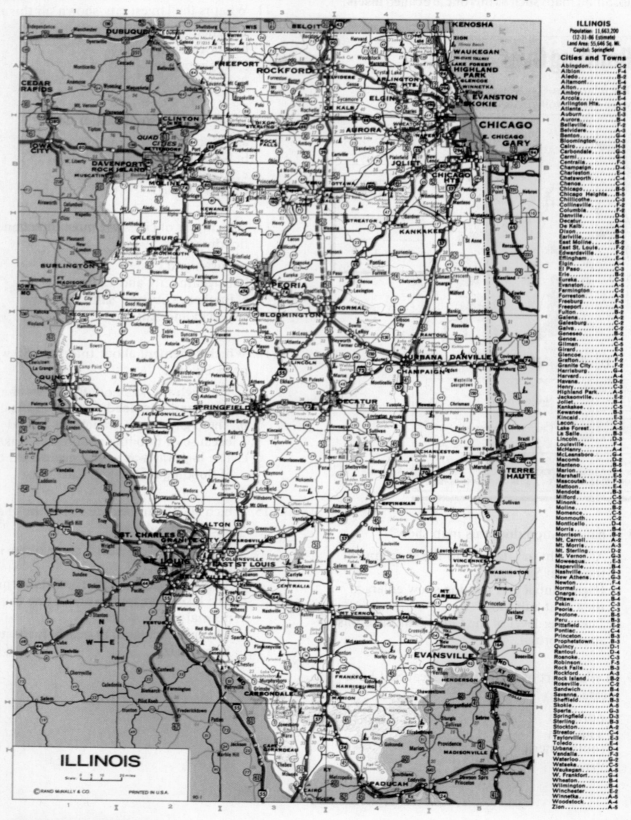

ILLINOIS
Population: 11,663,200
(12-31-86 Estimate)
Land Area: 55,646 Sq. Mi.
Capital: Springfield

**Cities and Towns**

| | |
|---|---|
| Abingdon | C-2 |
| Albion | F-4 |
| Aledo | B-2 |
| Altamont | E-4 |
| Alton | F-2 |
| Amboy | B-3 |
| Arcola | E-4 |
| Arlington Hts. | A-4 |
| Atlanta | D-4 |
| Auburn | E-3 |
| Aurora | B-4 |
| Belleville | F-2 |
| Belvidere | A-4 |
| Benton | G-3 |
| Bloomington | D-3 |
| Cairo | H-3 |
| Carbondale | G-3 |
| Carmi | G-4 |
| Centralia | F-3 |
| Champaign | D-4 |
| Charleston | E-4 |
| Chatsworth | C-4 |
| Chenoa | C-4 |
| Chicago | B-5 |
| Chicago Heights | B-5 |
| Chillicothe | C-3 |
| Collinsville | F-2 |
| Columbia | F-2 |
| Danville | D-5 |
| Decatur | E-3 |
| De Kalb | A-4 |
| Dixon | B-3 |
| Earlville | B-4 |
| East Moline | B-2 |
| East St. Louis | F-2 |
| Edwardsville | F-2 |
| Effingham | E-4 |
| Elgin | A-4 |
| El Paso | C-3 |
| Erie | B-2 |
| Eureka | C-3 |
| Evanston | A-5 |
| Farmington | C-2 |
| Forreston | A-3 |
| Freeburg | F-3 |
| Freeport | A-3 |
| Fulton | B-2 |
| Galena | A-2 |
| Galesburg | C-2 |
| Galva | C-2 |
| Geneseo | B-2 |
| Genoa | A-4 |
| Gilman | C-5 |
| Girard | E-3 |
| Glencoe | A-5 |
| Grafton | F-2 |
| Granite City | F-2 |
| Harrisburg | G-4 |
| Harvard | A-4 |
| Havana | D-2 |
| Henry | C-3 |
| Highland Park | A-5 |
| Jacksonville | E-2 |
| Joliet | B-4 |
| Kankakee | C-5 |
| Kewanee | C-2 |
| Kincaid | E-3 |
| Lacon | C-3 |
| Lake Forest | A-5 |
| La Salle | B-3 |
| Lincoln | D-3 |
| Louisville | F-4 |
| McHenry | A-4 |
| McLeansboro | G-4 |
| Macomb | D-2 |
| Manteno | B-4 |
| Marion | G-4 |
| Marshall | E-5 |
| Mattoon | E-4 |
| Mendota | B-3 |
| Milford | C-5 |
| Minonk | C-3 |
| Moline | B-2 |
| Momence | C-5 |
| Monmouth | C-2 |
| Monticello | D-4 |
| Morris | B-4 |
| Morrison | B-2 |
| Mt. Carroll | A-2 |
| Mt. Morris | A-3 |
| Mt. Sterling | D-2 |
| Mt. Vernon | F-3 |
| Moweaqua | E-3 |
| Naperville | B-4 |
| Nashville | F-3 |
| New Athens | G-3 |
| Newton | F-4 |
| Normal | C-4 |
| Onarga | C-4 |
| Ottawa | B-4 |
| Pekin | C-3 |
| Peoria | C-3 |
| Peotone | B-4 |
| Peru | B-3 |
| Pittsfield | E-2 |
| Pontiac | C-4 |
| Princeton | B-3 |
| Prophetstown | B-2 |
| Quincy | D-1 |
| Rantoul | D-4 |
| Roanoke | C-3 |
| Robinson | F-5 |
| Rock Falls | B-3 |
| Rockford | A-3 |
| Rock Island | B-2 |
| Roseville | C-2 |
| Sandwich | B-4 |
| Savanna | A-2 |
| Sheffield | B-3 |
| Skokie | A-5 |
| Sparta | G-3 |
| Springfield | D-3 |
| Sterling | B-3 |
| Stockton | A-2 |
| Streator | C-4 |
| Taylorville | E-3 |
| Toledo | E-4 |
| Urbana | D-4 |
| Vandalia | F-3 |
| Waterloo | G-2 |
| Watseka | C-5 |
| Waukegan | A-5 |
| W. Frankfort | G-4 |
| Wheaton | B-4 |
| Wilmington | B-4 |
| Winchester | E-2 |
| Winnetka | A-5 |
| Woodstock | A-4 |
| Zion | A-5 |

When you are planning a trip, a highway map can help you choose the best route. If you are in a hurry, you will want the fastest route. If your car is low on gasoline, you need to know the shortest route. If you are on vacation, you may want a route with interesting places to visit. If you must arrive at your destination by a certain time, you need to know how long it takes to drive from one city to another.

Use the highway map of Illinois to answer the following questions. Use the index to locate cities and towns. For small towns that are not listed in the index, grid references are given in parentheses in the question.

1. What direction would you travel to go from Chicago to Springfield on Interstate 55?

   a. northwest      c. southeast
   b. southwest      d. northeast

2. Which two cities are the farthest distance apart?

   a. Peoria and Galesburg
   b. Decatur and Urbana
   c. Springfield and East St. Louis
   d. Bloomington and Urbana

3. What is the shortest route from the south side of Chicago to St. Louis, Missouri (F-2)?

   a. Take Interstate 57 south to Interstate 70. Go east on Interstate 70 to St. Louis.
   b. Take Interstate 57 south to Interstate 72. Go west on Interstate 72 to Interstate 55 at Springfield. Turn south on Interstate 55 to St. Louis.
   c. Take Interstate 80 west to Interstate 55. Go south on Interstate 55 through Springfield to St. Louis.

4. Heidi lives in East St. Louis. She has a job interview in Decatur at 1:30 p.m. She will travel by interstate highway all the way. The speed limit is 65 miles per hour. What time must she leave home to be on time for her interview?

   a. 11:10 a.m.      c. 12:00 noon
   b. 12:30 p.m.      d. 11:50 a.m.

5. Which city is at the junction of the Mississippi and Ohio rivers?

   a. Granite City      c. Peoria
   b. Moline      d. Cairo

6. Henry is going from Peoria to Urbana. He must make a stop in Springfield on the way. What is the shortest route for him to take?

   a. Go southeast on Interstate 74 to Urbana. Take Interstate 72 southwest to Springfield. Go northeast on Interstate 72 to Urbana.
   b. Go southeast on Interstate 74 to Interstate 55. Turn southwest on Interstate 55 to Springfield. Go northeast on Interstate 72 to Urbana.
   c. Go southeast on Interstate 74 to U.S. Highway 51. Take Highway 51 south to Interstate 72. Go west on Interstate 72 to Springfield. Go northeast on Interstate 72 to Urbana.

7. Which city lies closest to the Shawnee National Forest?

   a. Rockford      c. Carbondale
   b. Decatur      d. Mt. Carmel

8. What river forms part of the eastern boundary of Illinois?

   a. Missouri      c. Mississippi
   b. Wabash      d. Illinois

9. What direction would you travel to go from Moline to Chicago on Interstate 80?

   a. west      c. south
   b. north      d. east

10. You are on vacation and have just visited Mark Twain's home in Hannibal, Missouri (E-1). You want to visit New Salem, near Springfield, Illinois, where Abraham Lincoln worked as a young man. You also want to visit Lincoln's home and tomb in Springfield and his log cabin near Charleston. Choose a route to reach these places from Hannibal and mark it on the map.

# Planning a Trip

**Objectives:** to choose routes, estimate travel times, and locate points of interest on a highway map

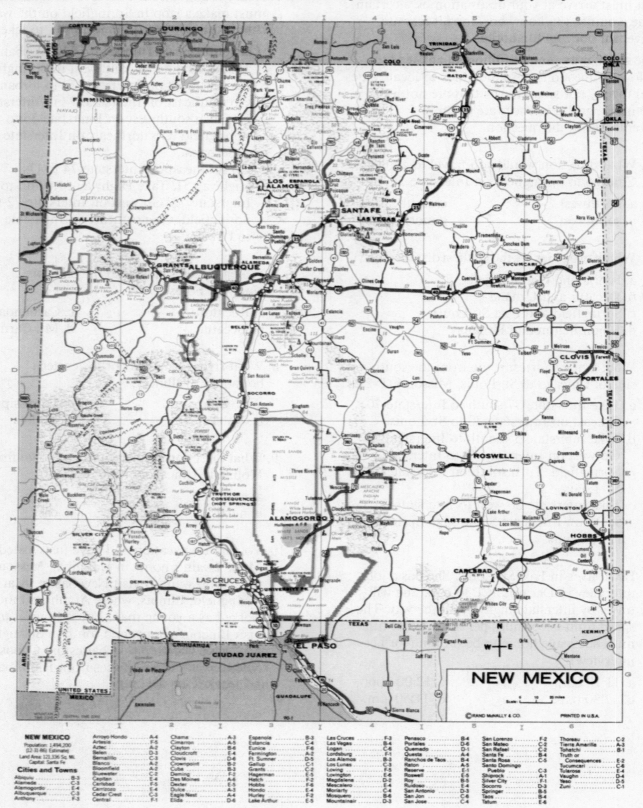

**NEW MEXICO**

Scale: 0    10    50 miles

© RAND McNALLY & CO.                    PRINTED IN U.S.A.

**NEW MEXICO**
Population: 1,494,200
(12-31-86) Estimate)
Land Area: 121,336 Sq. Mi.
Capital: Santa Fe

**Cities and Towns**

| | | | | | | |
|---|---|---|---|---|---|---|
| Abiquiu .......... B-3 | Chama .......... A-3 | Espanola .......... B-3 | Las Cruces .......... F-3 | Penasco .......... B-4 | San Lorenzo .......... F-2 | Thoreau .......... C-2 |
| Alameda .......... C-3 | Artesia .......... F-5 | Cimarron .......... A-5 | Estancia .......... C-4 | Las Vegas .......... B-4 | Portales .......... D-6 | San Mateo .......... C-2 | Tierra Amarilla .......... A-3 |
| Alamogordo .......... E-3 | Aztec .......... A-2 | Clayton .......... B-6 | Eunice .......... F-6 | Logan .......... B-5 | Quemado .......... D-1 | San Rafael .......... C-2 | Tohatchi .......... B-1 |
| Albuquerque .......... C-3 | Belen .......... D-3 | Cloudcroft .......... E-4 | Farmington .......... A-2 | Lordsburg .......... F-1 | Questa .......... A-4 | Santa Fe .......... B-4 | Truth or |
| Anthony .......... F-3 | Bernalillo .......... C-3 | Clovis .......... D-6 | Ft. Sumner .......... D-5 | Los Alamos .......... B-3 | Rancho de Taos .......... B-4 | Santa Rosa .......... C-5 | Consequences .......... E-2 |
| | Blanco .......... A-2 | Crownpoint .......... B-2 | Gallup .......... C-1 | Los Lunas .......... C-3 | Raton .......... A-5 | Santo Domingo | Tucumcari .......... C-6 |
| | Bloomfield .......... A-2 | Cuba .......... B-3 | Grants .......... C-2 | Loving .......... F-5 | Reserve .......... E-1 | Pueblo .......... C-3 | Tularosa .......... E-4 |
| | Bluewater .......... C-2 | Deming .......... F-2 | Hagerman .......... E-5 | Lovington .......... E-6 | Roswell .......... E-5 | Shiprock .......... A-1 | Vaughn .......... D-4 |
| | Capitan .......... E-4 | Des Moines .......... A-6 | Hatch .......... E-2 | Magdalena .......... D-2 | Roy .......... B-5 | Silver City .......... F-1 | Yeso .......... D-5 |
| | Carlsbad .......... F-5 | Dexter .......... E-5 | Hobbs .......... F-6 | Mescalero .......... E-4 | Ruidoso .......... E-4 | Socorro .......... D-3 | Zuni .......... C-1 |
| | Carrizozo .......... E-4 | Dulce .......... A-3 | Hondo .......... E-4 | Moriarty .......... C-4 | San Antonio .......... D-3 | Springer .......... B-5 | |
| | Cedar Crest .......... C-3 | Eagle Nest .......... A-4 | Hurley .......... F-2 | Mosquero .......... B-6 | San Jon .......... C-6 | Taos .......... B-4 | |
| | Central .......... F-1 | Elida .......... D-6 | Lake Arthur .......... E-5 | Mountainair .......... D-3 | San Jose .......... C-4 | Tatum .......... E-4 | |

Use the highway map of New Mexico to answer the following questions. Use the index to locate cities and towns.

1. What direction would you travel if you went from Albuquerque to Las Cruces on Interstate 25?

   a. north
   b. south
   c. east
   d. west

2. Taking the most direct route, which two cities are the shortest distance apart?

   a. Belen and Socorro
   b. Raton and Tucumcari
   c. Gallup and Grants
   d. Deming and Truth or Consequences

3. If you wanted to take a trip from Santa Fe through some national forests, which route should you choose?

   a. Take Highway 84 north from Santa Fe.
   b. Take Interstate 25 southwest from Santa Fe.
   c. Take Highway 41 south from Santa Fe.
   d. Take Highway 285 south from Santa Fe.

4. Suppose you are in Santa Fe and you want to drive to Tucumcari. Your goal is to drive as few miles as possible. Which route should you choose?

   a. Take Interstate 25 southwest to Albuquerque. Then go east on Interstate 40 to Tucumcari.
   b. Take Interstate 25 east to Highway 84. Go south on Highway 84 to Interstate 40. Take Interstate 40 east to Tucumcari.
   c. Take Interstate 25 southwest to Highway 60. Go east on Highway 60 to Highway 84. Take Highway 84 north to Interstate 40, and follow Interstate 40 to Tucumcari.

5. Suppose you wanted to drive along the Rio Grande for about 200 miles. Which highway should you choose?

   a. Highway 185
   b. Interstate 10
   c. Interstate 25
   d. Highway 187

6. Which highway would take you from border to border across New Mexico in the fewest miles?

   a. Interstate 25
   b. Highway 60
   c. Highway 84
   d. Interstate 40

7. Which one of the following states borders New Mexico on the east?

   a. Arizona
   b. Oklahoma
   c. Colorado
   d. Utah

8. You are planning to drive from Las Cruces to Roswell on Highway 70. If you can drive at an average speed of 60 miles per hour, about how long will the trip take?

   a. 2 hours and 40 minutes
   b. 3 hours and 30 minutes
   c. 1 hour and 40 minutes
   d. 2 hours and 20 minutes

9. Find the Continental Divide on the map and trace its route. Which one of the following statements about the divide is correct?

   a. No highway crosses the Continental Divide.
   b. The Continental Divide does not run through any Indian reservations.
   c. No river runs through the Continental Divide.
   d. The Continental Divide does not run through any national forests.

10. Suppose you are in Las Cruces. You want to visit White Sands National Monument, the Living Desert, and Carlsbad Caverns National Park. Mark the most direct route for your trip on the map.

Museum of Fine Arts in Santa Fe, New Mexico

# Analyzing a Trend

**Objective:** to use information on a map to analyze a trend or development

In 1920, the Twentieth Amendment to the U.S. Constitution granted women in the United States the right to vote. Before that time, women usually could vote for the president but not for other officials. In many states, women could not vote at all.

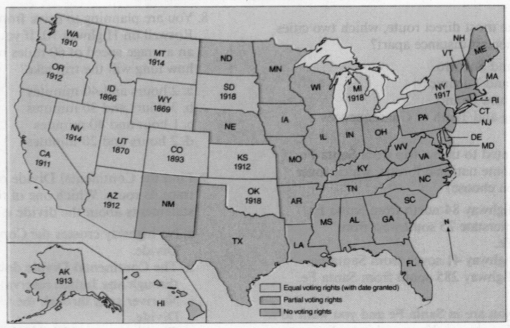

**VOTING RIGHTS FOR WOMEN BEFORE 1920**

1. Which one of the following states granted women equal voting rights before 1920?

   a. New Mexico     c. Ohio
   b. Maine     d. Wyoming

2. Which one of the following states granted women partial voting rights?

   a. Texas     c. California
   b. Florida     d. Delaware

3. What was the first state to grant women equal voting rights?

   a. New York     c. Wyoming
   b. Utah     d. Maine

4. How many states granted women equal voting rights before 1900?

   a. sixteen     c. twelve
   b. four     d. one

5. In what part of the country were women most likely to have equal voting rights?

   a. northeast     c. midwest
   b. southeast     d. west

6. In what part of the country were women least likely to have any voting rights?

   a. northeast     c. midwest
   b. southeast     d. west

7. Which statement best describes the trend in voting rights for women.

   a. Voting rights for women began in the midwestern states and spread gradually to other parts of the country.
   b. Voting rights for women began in the western states and spread to the midwest.
   c. Voting rights for women began in the southeast and spread to the midwest and the west.

# Solving a Land-Use Problem

**Objective:** to analyze map data and choose the best location or solve a problem

City planners use detailed maps to choose locations for new building projects. Such projects can include new highways, dams, shopping malls, and office centers. Use the map below to answer the questions.

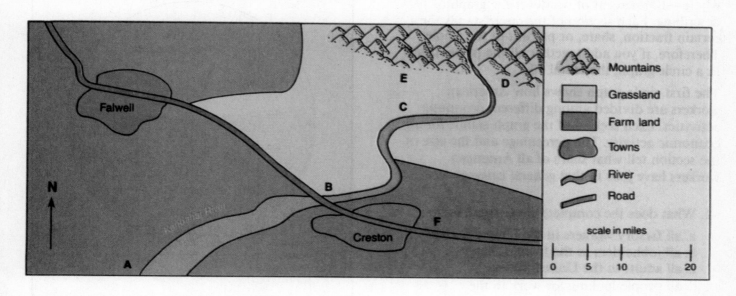

1. The Kandahar River flows southwest. It floods nearly every year. Which town probably suffers the most damage from these floods?

   a. Creston            b. Falwell

2. The citizens have decided to build a dam on the river to help control the floods. The dam will create a lake on its upstream side. The people want to place the dam so that it protects the areas where they live. However, they do not want the lake to cover their valuable farm land. Which point on the river would be best for building the dam?

   a. point A        c. point C
   b. point B        d. point D

3. Which point on the map would probably be covered by water after the dam was built?

   a. point B        c. point F
   b. point E        d. point A

4. Give three reasons explaining why the point you chose would be the best one for the dam.

   (a)_____
   _____
   (b)_____
   _____
   (c)_____
   _____

5. People in Creston and Falwell hope to use the new lake as a recreation area. What must they build before they can do so?

   a. a road from point B to the point where the dam is built
   b. a group of cabins in the mountains near point D
   c. a highway from Falwell to point A
   d. a set of boat docks at Creston

# Reading a Circle Graph

**Objectives:** to use information on a circle graph to make comparisons and draw inferences

A circle graph shows how something is divided into parts. The complete circle stands for the whole—100 percent of whatever the graph is describing. Each section of the circle stands for a certain fraction, share, or percent of the whole. Therefore, if you add together all the percentages in a circle graph, they total 100.

The first circle graph shows how American workers are divided among different economic activities. Each section of the graph stands for an economic activity. The percentage and the size of the section tell what share of all American workers have jobs in that general category.

### WORKERS IN THE UNITED STATES

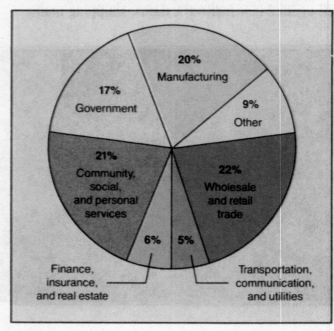

1. What does the complete circle stand for?

   a. all factory workers in the United States
   b. all jobholders in the United States
   c. all adults in the United States
   d. all people looking for work in the United States

2. What percentage of all people who work have jobs in government?

   a. 17%   b. 21%   c. 22%   d. 9%

3. Which category of jobs employs the most people in the United States?

   a. transportation, communications, and utilities
   b. community, social, and personal services
   c. wholesale and retail trade
   d. government

4. Which category of jobs employs the smallest percentage of people?

   a. transportation, communications, and utilities
   b. wholesale and retail trade
   c. finance, insurance, and real estate
   d. manufacturing

5. Which two categories together employ the same percentage of workers as the wholesale and retail trade?

   a. manufacturing together with government
   b. community, social, and personal services together with finance, insurance, and real estate
   c. finance, insurance, and real estate together with other
   d. government together with transportation, communications, and utilities

6. Based on the information in the graph, what action would probably cause the most people to lose their jobs?

   a. a large cut in the building industry
   b. a large decrease in buying goods by the public
   c. a cut in government spending
   d. a decrease in air travel in the country

A drawing can work in the same way as a circle graph, even if it is not shaped like a circle. This drawing shows the sources of income for all elderly people in the United States. The graph shows income for the elderly as a group. An elderly person might have income from one or more of these sources.

The graph uses some special terms. **Assets** include the money a person has saved or invested and the property they own. A **pension** is a regular payment, usually from a retired person's former employer. Social Security and Railroad Retirement are national pension programs set up by law in the 1930s. Nearly all workers and employers contribute money to one of these programs.

## USA SNAPSHOTS

A look at statistics that shape our finances

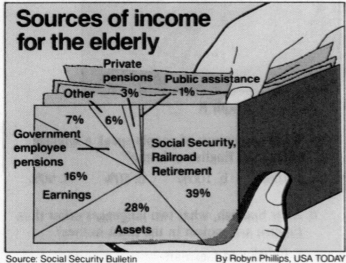

### Sources of income for the elderly

Private pensions 3%
Public assistance 1%
Other 7%
6%
Government employee pensions 16%
Earnings 28%
Social Security, Railroad Retirement 39%
Assets

Source: Social Security Bulletin        By Robyn Phillips, USA TODAY

7. What source provides the largest share of income for elderly people in the United States?
   a. assets (savings, investments)
   b. Social Security and Railroad Retirement
   c. government employee pensions
   d. earnings

8. What percentage of income do private pensions provide for the elderly?
   a. 7%   b. 6%   c. 3%   d. 39%

9. What percentage of income comes from elderly people's own assets (savings, investments, and property)?
   a. 7%   b. 39%   c. 16%   d. 28%

10. What percentage of elderly people's income does public assistance (welfare programs) provide?
    a. 3%   b. 1%   c. 7%   d. 40%

11. What percentage of their income do elderly people provide for themselves through their earnings and their assets?
    a. 39%   b. 11%   c. 44%   d. 16%

12. What percentage of elderly people's income comes from other sources?
    a. 3%   b. 7%   c. 6%   d. 16%

13. What change would probably be of least concern to the elderly?
    a. Government employee pensions are canceled.
    b. Public assistance programs for the elderly are stopped.
    c. Elderly people are not permitted to work.
    d. Other sources of income are no longer available.

14. Which change would probably cause the greatest hardship among the elderly?
    a. The Social Security and Railroad Retirement funds of the government go bankrupt.
    b. Both government pensions and pensions from private companies are stopped.
    c. People are not allowed to work after age 60.
    d. Public assistance programs for the elderly are stopped.

# Comparing Circle Graphs

**Objectives:** to compare circle graphs and draw conclusions based on the information in the graphs

People in the United States speak many languages. They may use one language at school or at work and another language at home with their families. These graphs give you information about the languages people speak in their homes. Use the graphs to answer the following questions.

**LANGUAGES SPOKEN AT HOME**

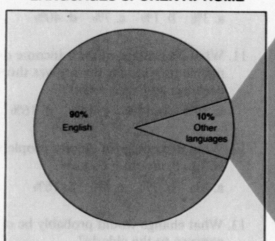

**Graph A**

**LANGUAGES OTHER THAN ENGLISH**

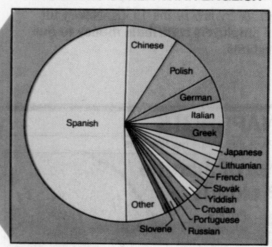

**Graph B**

1. Which graph shows languages other than English spoken at home by people in the United States?

   a. Graph A          b. Graph B

2. What language do most people in the United States speak at home?

   a. Spanish          c. English
   b. Chinese          d. Polish

3. What percentage of people speak English at home?

   a. 10%   b. 100%   c. 50%   d. 90%

4. Of the people who speak a language other than English at home, about what part speak Spanish?

   a. one fourth          c. one tenth
   b. one third           d. one half

5. What percentage of people speak a language other than English at home?

   a. 10%   b. 100%   c. 50%   d. 90%

6. After Spanish, what two languages other than English are spoken in the most homes?

   a. Polish and German
   b. Chinese and Polish
   c. Italian and German
   d. Greek and Chinese

7. Which one of the following languages would be included in the "other" category on Graph B?

   a. Yiddish          c. Korean
   b. German           d. English

8. Based on the information on both graphs, about what percentage of people in the United States speak Spanish at home?

   a. 5%   b. 50%   c. 10%   d. 25%

# Reading a Bar Graph

**Objectives:** to interpret information from a bar graph and to draw conclusions based on that information

A bar graph has two axes: a horizontal axis, along the bottom and a vertical axis, along the side. The label on each axis tells you what that axis measures or compares.

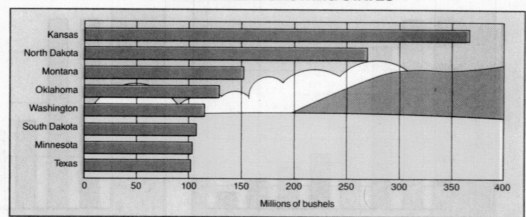

**LEADING WHEAT-GROWING STATES**

Kansas
North Dakota
Montana
Oklahoma
Washington
South Dakota
Minnesota
Texas

0    50   100   150   200   250   300   350   400

Millions of bushels

1. Which state produced the most wheat?

   a. Minnesota
   b. Kansas
   c. North Dakota
   d. Oklahoma

2. What does the horizontal axis on this graph measure?

   a. acres of land used to grow wheat
   b. dollars earned by sales of wheat
   c. bushels of wheat grown
   d. number of farmers who raise wheat

3. About how many million bushels of wheat were grown in North Dakota?

   a. 350   b. 220   c. 400   d. 270

4. Which state produced less wheat than Minnesota?

   a. Washington          c. Texas
   b. South Dakota        d. Oklahoma

5. About how much more wheat did Montana produce than Minnesota?

   a. about 10 million bushels
   b. about 130 million bushels
   c. about 50 million bushels
   d. about 100 million bushels

6. Based on the information in this graph, which generalization about wheat growing is true?

   a. The climate and soil in South Dakota and Minnesota are not good for growing wheat.
   b. The climate and soil in Kansas and North Dakota are very good for growing wheat.
   c. No wheat is raised in Georgia and Louisiana.
   d. The United States is one of the world's leading wheat producers.

7. About how many bushels of wheat did Oklahoma produce?

   a. 100 million          c. 220 thousand
   b. 130 thousand         d. 130 million

8. What can you infer from the information in this graph?

   a. Most wheat in the United States is grown in the midwestern states.
   b. Wheat is grown equally in all parts of the United States.
   c. Most wheat in the United States is grown in the far western part of the country.
   d. Wheat is grown generally in the eastern states.

# Comparing Bar Graphs

**Objectives:** to compare information from two bar graphs and draw conclusions

**CORN PRODUCTION**

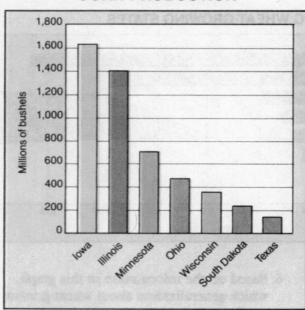

**SOYBEAN PRODUCTION**

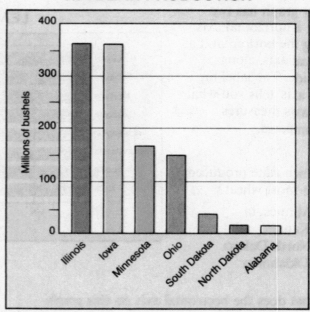

Compare the graphs and answer the questions. Be sure to check labels on the axes.

1. Which two states were leading producers of both corn and soybeans?

 a. Iowa and Illinois
 b. Illinois and Minnesota
 c. Iowa and Minnesota
 d. Iowa and Ohio

2. Of the states shown, which one produced small amounts of both corn and soybeans?

 a. South Dakota     c. Illinois
 b. Iowa            d. Texas

3. About how much corn was harvested in Iowa, according to the graph?

 a. almost 1 billion, 800 million bushels
 b. almost 1 billion, 650 million bushels
 c. about 1 million, 300 thousand bushels
 d. about 1 million, 650 thousand bushels

4. About how many bushels of soybeans were harvested in Ohio?

 a. 150 thousand     c. 190 thousand
 b. 190 million      d. 150 million

5. How does the production of corn compare with the production of soybeans in these states?

 a. Most states produce about the same amount of corn and soybeans.
 b. Most states produce much more corn than soybeans.
 c. Most states produce much more soybeans than corn.

6. Which state would be hurt the least by a drop in the price of corn?

 a. Wisconsin       c. Illinois
 b. Minnesota      d. Texas

7. Which state's prosperity probably depends most on growing corn and soybeans?

 a. Ohio          c. South Dakota
 b. Minnesota     d. Iowa

# Reading a Double-Bar Graph

**Objectives:** to gather information, make comparisons, and draw conclusions
based on data presented in a double-bar graph

A **double-bar graph** allows you to compare two
different categories of information using the
same units of measurement. For example, on the
graph below both categories are measured in acres.

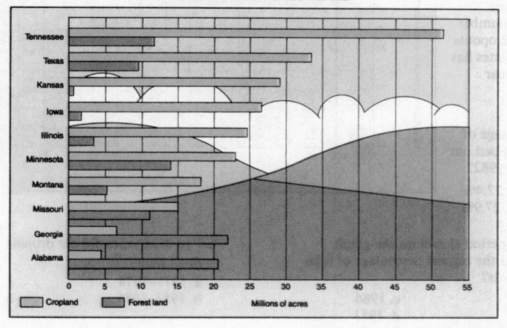

**CROPLAND AND FOREST LAND**

1. Which state shown on the graph has the most
   acres of forest land?

   a. Tennessee          c. Texas
   b. Georgia            d. Alabama

2. About how many acres of land are used for
   growing crops in Montana?

   a. 15 million acres
   b. 6 million acres
   c. 18 million acres
   d. 20 million acres

3. Which two kinds of information could you
   show on a double-bar graph like this one?

   a. acres of forest and board feet of lumber
   b. miles of highways and miles of railroads
   c. acres of cropland and tons of corn
   d. tons of coal and barrels of oil

4. Which state has almost no forest land?

   a. Texas              c. Kansas
   b. Georgia            d. Alabama

5. Based on the information in this graph,
   which conclusion about forest land in the
   midwestern states is correct?

   a. There are no forests in the Midwest.
   b. Forests are far more widespread than
      cropland in the midwest.
   c. There are very large forests in the Midwest.
   d. Cropland is far more widespread than
      forest land in the Midwest.

6. Which state has almost the same amount of
   cropland and forest land?

   a. Alabama            c. Montana
   b. Texas              d. Missouri

# Reading a Line Graph

**Objectives:** to find and interpret information on a single-line graph

A line graph has a horizontal axis and a vertical axis. It can show how something changes over time. The line graph on this page shows how the number of high school dropouts in the United States has changed from year to year.

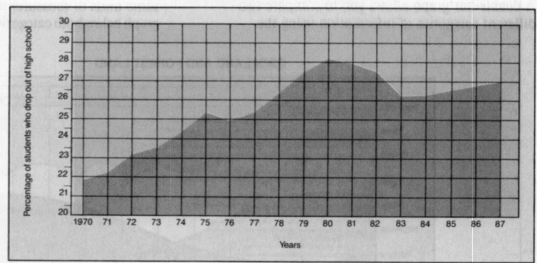

**HIGH SCHOOL DROP-OUT RATES**

1. What percentage of students dropped out of school in 1982?

   a. 28%      c. 27.4%
   b. 25%      d. 27.9%

2. For the time period shown on the graph, what year had the highest percentage of high school dropouts?

   a. 1980                c. 1986
   b. 1976                d. 1981

3. What year had the lowest dropout rate for the time period shown on the graph?

   a. 1986                c. 1970
   b. 1983                d. 1976

4. What does the vertical axis of this graph measure?

   a. millions of students who drop out
   b. millions of students who graduate
   c. the percentage of students who drop out
   d. the percentage of students who graduate

5. How did the dropout rate change between 1980 and 1983?

   a. It increased about 2%.
   b. It decreased about 2%.
   c. It increased about 20%.
   d. It decreased about 20%.

6. For what years did the dropout rate increase most rapidly?

   a. 1977–1979           c. 1980–1982
   b. 1983–1985           d. 1979–1981

7. Which statement is true according to this graph?

   a. Each year at least 30% of students have dropped out.
   b. The only years the drop-out rate fell below 23% was 1970 and 1971.
   c. Each year at least 23% of students have dropped out.

8. Based on the information in the graph, what can you predict about the percentage of high school dropouts in the 1990s?

   a. It will be lower than it has ever been.
   b. It will be higher than it has ever been.
   c. It will probably be about the same as in 1987.
   d. It will probably be higher than it was in 1987.

# Reading a Double-Line Graph

**Objectives:** to interpret a double-line graph and make comparisons and generalizations based on the information

On a double-line graph, you can compare two kinds of information. The graph on this page gives information about money.

One line shows the inflation rate. The inflation rate measures the increases in the average paid for goods and services.

The other line shows the interest rate. **Interest** is the money a borrower has to pay a lender in addition to the amount borrowed.

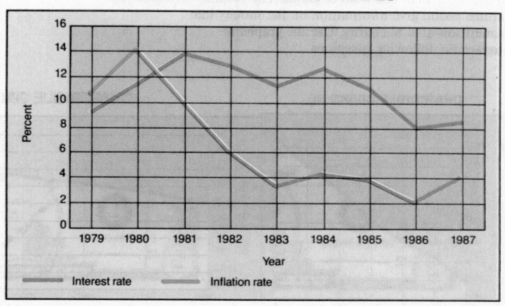

**INFLATION AND INTEREST RATES**

1. What was the inflation rate in 1982?

    a. 3%   b. 13%   c. 6%   d. 10%

2. In what year did interest rates reach their highest point?

    a. 1980                   c. 1986
    b. 1981                   d. 1987

3. What was the interest rate in 1986?

    a. 8%   b. 2%   c. 4%   d. 11%

4. During what year did the inflation rate begin to rise after a long decline?

    a. 1980–1981              c. 1983–1984
    b. 1985–1986              d. 1982–1983

5. What can you conclude from this graph?

    a. Interest rates are usually lower than inflation rates.
    b. Interest and inflation rates are usually the same.
    c. Interest rates are usually higher than inflation rates.

6. In 1986, what was the difference between the interest rate and the inflation rate?

    a. The interest rate was 6% higher.
    b. The inflation rate was 6% higher.
    c. The interest rate was 8% higher.
    d. The inflation rate was 8% higher.

7. What can you infer about changes in interest and inflation rates?

    a. If inflation decreases, interest rates will also decrease.
    b. If inflation increases, interest rates will decrease.
    c. If inflation increases, interest rates will not change.
    d. If inflation decreases, interest rates cannot be predicted.

8. When were the interest and inflation rates briefly at the same level?

    a. 1979–1980              c. 1983–1984
    b. 1980–1981              d. 1986–1987

# Interpreting Graphs

**Objectives:** to gather information, draw conclusions, and interpret the point-of-view in graphs

Sometimes the best way to present information is to use more than one kind of graph. The graphs in this lesson give information on the money that Americans give to charity. Use the graphs to answer the following questions.

**CHARITABLE GIVING (A)**

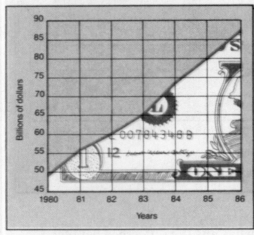

**CHARITABLE GIVING (B)**

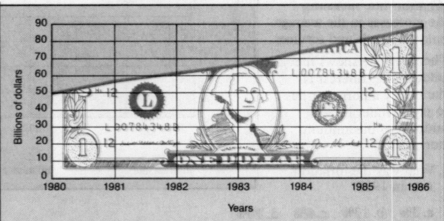

1. According to graph A, how much money did Americans donate in 1982?

   a. about $80 billion
   b. about $60 billion
   c. about $70 million
   d. about $55 billion

2. According to graph B, how much money did Americans donate in 1982?

   a. about $70 million
   b. about $80 billion
   c. about $55 billion
   d. about $60 billion

3. Which graph gives the impression that donations to charity are rising rapidly?

   a. graph A                     b. graph B

4. What is the difference between graphs A and B on charitable giving?

   a. Both graphs present the same information, but graph B begins at zero dollars.
   b. Graph A shows more money given to charity than graph B.
   c. The two graphs cover different years.

5. What impression does graph B give?

   a. Donations have decreased since 1980.
   b. Donations have increased gradually since 1980.
   c. Donations have remained the same since 1980.
   d. Donations increased between 1980 and 1983 but then began to decrease.

## WHERE DONATIONS WENT IN 1985 (C)

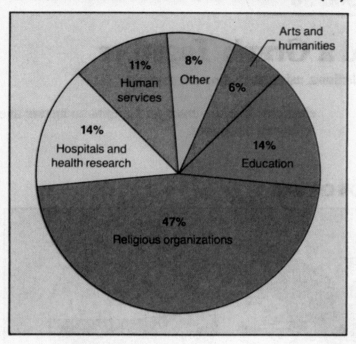

- 11% Human services
- 8% Other
- Arts and humanities
- 6%
- 14% Hospitals and health research
- 14% Education
- 47% Religious organizations

6. Which person would be most likely to use graph A in a newspaper or magazine?

a. the leader of a charity who is asking for more donations
b. a person who wants to prove that charities have plenty of money
c. a person who wants to compare charities in the United States with those in other countries
d. a person who wants to show that Americans give little to charity

7. Which type of charity on graph C received the most money from donations in 1985?

a. education
b. human services
c. arts and humanities
d. religious organizations

8. What percentage of charitable donations in 1985 went to religious organizations?

a. 14%
b. 11%
c. 47%
d. 6%

9. Based on the graphs, about how much money did religious organizations receive in 1985?

a. about $38 billion
b. about $79 billion
c. about $50 billion
d. about $14 billion

10. About how much money was donated to human services in 1985?

a. about $11 billion
b. about $8.8 billion
c. about $11 million
d. about $8.1 million

11. About how much money did arts and humanities receive in 1980?

a. about $3.1 billion
b. about $6.2 billion
c. It is impossible to tell from the information on these graphs.

12. Which two groups received the same percentage of donations in 1985?

a. hospitals and education
b. hospitals and human services
c. human services and education
d. education and arts

Former president Jimmy Carter pitches in on Habitat for Humanity projects fixing and building houses for the homeless.

# Using a Map and a Graph Together

**Objectives:** to compare and analyze information on elections, using maps and circle graphs

Reading a map and a graph together can give you more information than either one alone. These maps and graphs show you the results of three elections. Use the maps and graphs to answer the following questions.

## ELECTION OF 1896

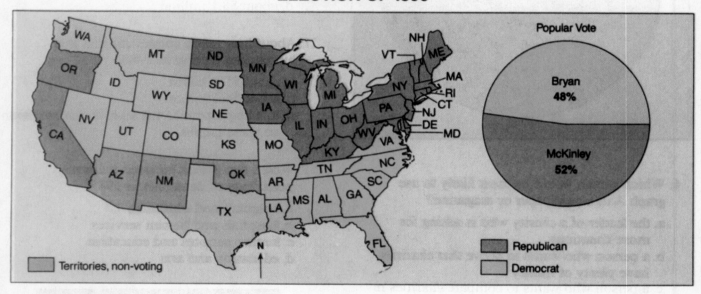

1. Which candidate won the election of 1964?

    a. William McKinley
    b. Ronald Reagan
    c. Lyndon Johnson
    d. Barry Goldwater

2. Which candidate won the state of Nebraska in 1896?

    a. James Earl Carter
    b. William Jennings Bryan
    c. Lyndon Johnson
    d. William McKinley

3. Which one of the following states did Lyndon Johnson win in 1964?

    a. Arizona
    b. Georgia
    c. South Carolina
    d. Iowa

4. In which election were some areas shown organized as territories instead of states?
    a. 1896   b. 1964   c. 1980

5. Which winning candidate had the highest percentage of the popular vote?

    a. William McKinley
    b. Lyndon Johnson
    c. Ronald Reagan
    d. James Earl Carter

6. In which election did the two candidates win about the same number of states?

    a. 1980   b. 1964   c. 1896

7. In which election did an independent candidate receive a share of the popular vote?

    a. 1896   b. 1964   c. 1980

## ELECTION OF 1964

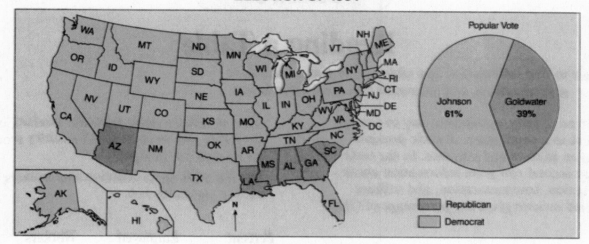

**Popular Vote**

Johnson 61%  Goldwater 39%

Republican
Democrat

## ELECTION OF 1980

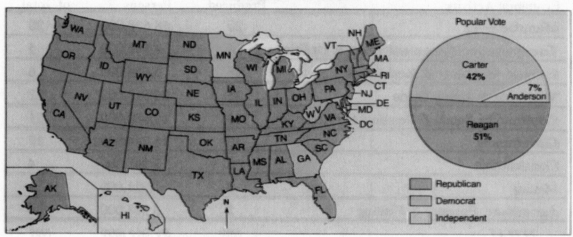

**Popular Vote**

Carter 42%  7% Anderson  Reagan 51%

Republican
Democrat
Independent

8. Which one of these candidates won the fewest states in any of the elections shown here?

a. Ronald Reagan
b. James Earl Carter
c. William McKinley
d. Lyndon Johnson

9. Where did Barry Goldwater receive his greatest support?

a. in the northeastern industrial states
b. in the midwestern farming states
c. in the far western states
d. in the deep southern states

10. Which candidate won a share of the popular vote but did not win any states?

a. Lyndon Johnson
b. John Anderson
c. William Jennings Bryan
d. James Earl Carter

11. Which winning candidate had the smallest share of the popular vote?

a. William McKinley
b. Lyndon Johnson
c. Ronald Reagan
d. John Anderson

12. What can you infer about the election of 1896?

a. William Jennings Bryan was popular in states where many people were farmers.
b. William McKinley was equally popular in all parts of the country.
c. Voter turnout was unusually low.
d. Neither candidate was able to win a majority of the votes.

13. Which elections might news reporters have described as landslides?

a. 1896 and 1964
b. 1896 and 1980
c. 1964 and 1980

# Reading a Table

**Objectives:** to find information in a table and to draw conclusions, generalizations, and inferences from that information

A **table** is an orderly, convenient way to present many facts in a small space. A table presents information in rows and columns. In the table below, the second *row* gives information about transportation, communication, and utilities. The second *column* gives the percentage of GDP.

**GDP** stands for gross domestic product, or all the goods and services that a country produces for its own use in a year.

Use the table on production and workers to answer questions 1–6.

| Economic Activity | Percent of GDP Produced | Employed Number of Persons | Workers Percent of Total |
|---|---|---|---|
| Manufacturing | 20 | 18,678,000 | 20 |
| Transportation, Communication & Utilities | 18 | 4,941,000 | 5 |
| Finance, Insurance & Real Estate | 16 | 5,454,000 | 6 |
| Wholesale & Retail Trade | 15 | 20,513,000 | 22 |
| Community, Social & Personal Services | 13 | 19,680,000 | 21 |
| Government | 10 | 15,744,000 | 17 |
| Construction | 3 | 3,947,000 | 4 |
| Mining | 3 | 1,021,000 | 1 |
| Agriculture, Forestry & Fishing | 2 | 3,383,000 | 4 |
| **TOTAL** | **100** | **93,361,000** | **100** |

1. Which economic activity employs the highest number of workers in the United States?

   a. manufacturing
   b. community, social, and personal services
   c. wholesale and retail trade
   d. mining

2. What percentage of the GDP comes from government?

   a. 17%   b. 10%   c. 21%   d. 14%

3. What percentage of the total work force works in community, social, and personal services?

   a. 20%   b. 13%   c. 22%   d. 21%

4. Based on the table, what economic activity produces the largest share of the GDP?

   a. mining
   b. transportation, communication, and utilities
   c. manufacturing
   d. community, social, and personal services

5. What percentage of the GDP comes from agriculture, forestry, and fishing?

   a. 2%   b. 4%   c. 22%   d. 12%

6. Based on the table, what activity employs 5,454,000 workers?

   a. mining
   b. wholesale & retail trade
   c. finance, insurance and real estate
   d. construction

The income gap column shows the difference (gap) between the dollar earnings of men and women.

Use the table on education and income to answer questions 7–15.

## INCOME IN RELATION TO EDUCATION

| Education (Years Completed) | Median Income* Women | Men | Income Gap in Dollars |
|---|---|---|---|
| Elementary school: | | | |
| Less than 8th grade | $10,153 | $14,485 | $4,332 |
| 8th grade | 11,183 | 18,541 | 7,358 |
| High school: | | | |
| 9th–11th grade | 12,267 | 20,003 | 7,736 |
| 12th grade | 15,947 | 24,701 | 8,754 |
| College: | | | |
| 1–3 years | 18,516 | 28,025 | 9,509 |
| 4 years or more | 24,482 | 36,665 | 12,183 |

(*The *median* is the middle of a group of numbers; half the people in each group make less than the median income, and half make more.)

7. What is the median income for women who left school after graduating from high school?

   a. $24,701
   b. $15,947
   c. $12,267
   d. $18,516

8. What is the median income for men who left school after finishing the eighth grade?

   a. $14,485
   b. $18,541
   c. $7,358
   d. $11,183

9. Which group earns the highest median income?

   a. women who completed high school
   b. men who completed eighth grade
   c. men who completed high school
   d. women who completed two years of college

10. How much does women's median income rise if they finish college instead of stopping school after graduating from high school?

   a. $8,535
   b. $15,947
   c. $24,482
   d. $8,754

11. According to this table, how much less is a man likely to earn if he drops out of school after tenth grade instead of getting two years of college education?

   a. $3,324
   b. $20,003
   c. $28,025
   d. $8,022

12. How much more is a man with a four-year college education likely to earn than a woman with the same education?

   a. $24,482
   b. $36,665
   c. $9,509
   d. $12,183

13. What is the income gap between men and women who have completed high school?

   a. $4,332
   b. $24,701
   c. $8,754
   d. $15,947

14. What is the highest income a man with a high school diploma is likely to earn?

   a. $24,701 per year
   b. $36,665 per year
   c. $43,627 per year
   d. It is impossible to tell from the information given.

15. Which statement about the earnings gap between men and women is correct?

   a. Women usually earn more than men, depending on how educated they are.
   b. The gap grows wider at higher levels of education for men and women.
   c. The gap grows smaller as both men and women complete more years of school.

# Reading a Time Line

**Objectives:** to identify dates of events, compare time spans, and make
generalizations based on information in a time line

A **time line** shows you when events took place.
On a time line, events are arranged in
**chronological order,** or in the order in which they
took place, from the earliest to the latest.

The space between each division on a time line
is called an **interval.**

Time lines can be horizontal or vertical. The first
time line is arranged horizontally. Use this time
line to answer questions 1–8.

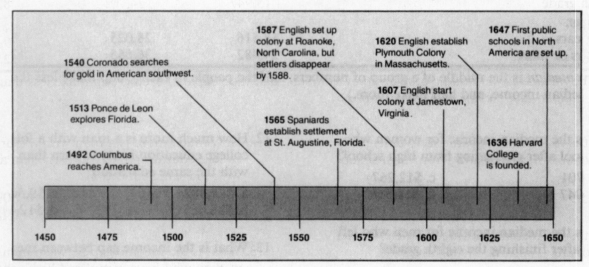

**1540** Coronado searches for gold in American southwest.

**1587** English set up colony at Roanoke, North Carolina, but settlers disappear by 1588.

**1620** English establish Plymouth Colony in Massachusetts.

**1647** First public schools in North America are set up.

**1513** Ponce de Leon explores Florida.

**1565** Spaniards establish settlement at St. Augustine, Florida.

**1607** English start colony at Jamestown, Virginia.

**1492** Columbus reaches America.

**1636** Harvard College is founded.

1450　1475　1500　1525　1550　1575　1600　1625　1650

1. What is the earliest date shown on the time line?

    a. 1400　b. 1500　c. 1450　d. 1650

2. How many years does the whole time line cover?

    a. 300　b. 200　c. 100　d. 1650

3. How many years does each interval on the
time line stand for?

    a. 100　b. 25　c. 50　d. 10

4. When did the Spaniard Francisco Vasquez de
Coronado search for gold in what is now the
southwestern United States?

    a. 1450　b. 1550　c. 1620　d. 1540

5. What was the earliest colony or settlement in
what is now the United States?

    a. Jamestown　　　c. St. Augustine
    b. Plymouth　　　　d. Roanoke

6. What event took place about 20 years after
Columbus discovered America?

    a. Ponce de Leon explored Florida.
    b. Coronado explored the American
    southwest.
    c. Jamestown was founded.
    d. Harvard College was founded.

7. In what year was Jamestown founded?

    a. 1585　b. 1620　c. 1607　d. 1600

8. Between what two events was the longest
span of time?

    a. Columbus's voyage and the exploration of
    Florida by Ponce de Leon
    b. the founding of Harvard College and the
    establishment of the first public schools
    c. Coronado's explorations and the founding
    of Roanoke
    d. the founding of Jamestown and the
    founding of Plymouth

This time line is arranged vertically. Use it to answer questions 9–16.

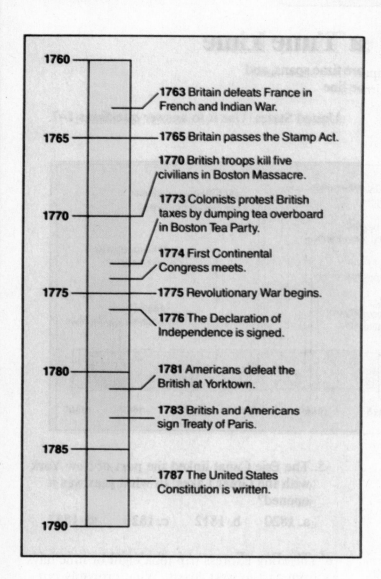

1760
**1763** Britain defeats France in French and Indian War.

1765
**1765** Britain passes the Stamp Act.

**1770** British troops kill five civilians in Boston Massacre.

1770
**1773** Colonists protest British taxes by dumping tea overboard in Boston Tea Party.

**1774** First Continental Congress meets.

1775
**1775** Revolutionary War begins.

**1776** The Declaration of Independence is signed.

1780
**1781** Americans defeat the British at Yorktown.

**1783** British and Americans sign Treaty of Paris.

1785

**1787** The United States Constitution is written.

1790

13. Which one of the following events took place between the Boston Massacre and the First Continental Congress?

a. the Boston Tea Party
b. the passage of the Stamp Act
c. the start of the Revolutionary War
d. the defeat of the British at Yorktown

14. How many years went by between the signing of the Declaration of Independence and the writing of the Constitution?

a. 21
b. 11
c. 6
d. 17

15. Based on the information in the time line, what can you tell about the Revolutionary War?

a. It ended before 1781.
b. It ended after 1787.
c. It ended between 1781 and 1783.
d. It ended between 1774 and 1775.

16. Which one of these conclusions seems correct for this period of American history?

a. There were many conflicts within a short period of time.
b. This was a fairly peaceful period.
c. This was a period of cooperation between Britain and the American colonies.
d. Very few important events occurred during these years.

9. How many years does this time line cover?

a. 1790    b. 25    c. 30    d. 1760

10. How many years does the space between each interval on the time line stand for?

a. 1    b. 50    c. 25    d. 5

11. In what year did the British win the French and Indian War?

a. 1765    b. 1763    c. 1700    d. 1770

12. In what year was the Treaty of Paris signed?

a. 1781    b. 1787    c. 1783    d. 1774

The Boston Tea Party of 1773 was a protest against British taxes on imported tea.

# Interpreting a Time Line

**Objectives:** to arrange events in chronological order, compare time spans, and
draw inferences based on information in a time line

This time line shows some major developments
in transportation and communication in the

United States. Use it to answer questions 1–7.

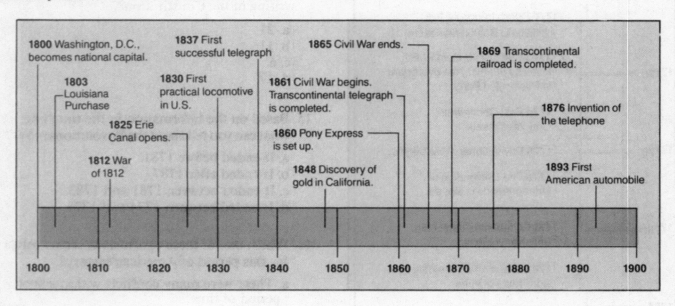

1. How many years does this time line cover?

    a. 1800    b. 1900    c. 200    d. 100

2. When was gold discovered in California?

    a. 1848    b. 1854    c. 1837    d. 1840

3. How many years went by between the
   building of the first practical locomotive and
   the completion of a railroad across the
   continent?

    a. 27    b. 52    c. 39    d. 12

4. Between what two events was the longest
   span of time?

    a. the first successful telegraph and the
       transcontinental telegraph
    b. the first practical locomotive and the first
       automobile
    c. the opening of the Erie Canal and the first
       successful telegraph
    d. the operation of Pony Express and the
       invention of the telephone

5. The Erie Canal linked the port of New York
   with the Great Lakes. In what year was it
   opened?

    a. 1820    b. 1812    c. 1825    d. 1837

6. The Pony Express trip took eight or nine days
   from east to west coasts. What probably put
   the Pony Express out of business?

    a. the invention of the first telegraph
    b. the invention of the telephone
    c. the transcontinental telegraph
    d. the invention of the automobile

7. What form of communication would have
   been the fastest way to let people on the east
   coast learn about gold being discovered in
   California?

    a. telephone
    b. transcontinental railroad
    c. Pony Express
    d. telegraph

This time line shows some events of the first half of the twentieth century. Use it to answer questions 8–13.

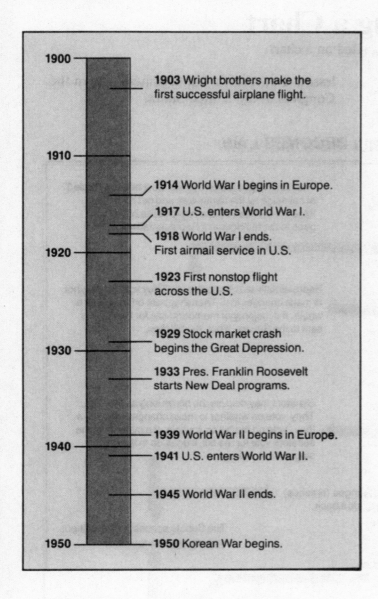

**1900**

**1903** Wright brothers make the first successful airplane flight.

**1910**

**1914** World War I begins in Europe.

**1917** U.S. enters World War I.

**1918** World War I ends.
First airmail service in U.S.

**1920**

**1923** First nonstop flight across the U.S.

**1929** Stock market crash begins the Great Depression.

**1930**

**1933** Pres. Franklin Roosevelt starts New Deal programs.

**1939** World War II begins in Europe.

**1940**

**1941** U.S. enters World War II.

**1945** World War II ends.

**1950**

**1950** Korean War begins.

8. In what year did the stock market crash occur?

  a. 1914        c. 1929
  b. 1941        d. 1933

9. In what year did the Wright brothers make the first successful airplane flight?

  a. 1930        c. 1914
  b. 1933        d. 1903

10. How many years went by between the end of World War I and the United States' entry into World War II?

  a. 31        c. 14
  b. 23        d. 4

11. Which one of the following periods is shortest?

  a. the period between the invention of the airplane and the first nonstop flight across the United States
  b. the period between the stock market crash and President Roosevelt's New Deal programs
  c. the period between the end of World War II and the beginning of the Korean War
  d. the period between the Wright brothers' first airplane flight and the beginning of airmail service

12. Which one of the following periods is not shown on the time line?

  a. the period between the invention of the airplane and the first nonstop flight across the United States
  b. the period between the stock market crash and President Roosevelt's New Deal programs
  c. the period between the end of World War II and the beginning of the Korean War
  d. the period between the Wright brothers' first airplane flight and the beginning of airmail service

13. Place the following events at the correct chronological point on the time line.

  a. 1927 Lindbergh made the first solo flight across the Atlantic.
  b. 1947 First supersonic flight
  c. 1941 First American jet flight
  d. 1911 First flight across the United States (in 68 hops)

# Reading a Chart

**Objectives:** to gather information and draw inferences based on a chart

Charts and diagrams combine words and pictures to present information. The chart in this lesson shows how a bill becomes a law in the Congress of the United States.

## HOW A FEDERAL BILL BECOMES LAW

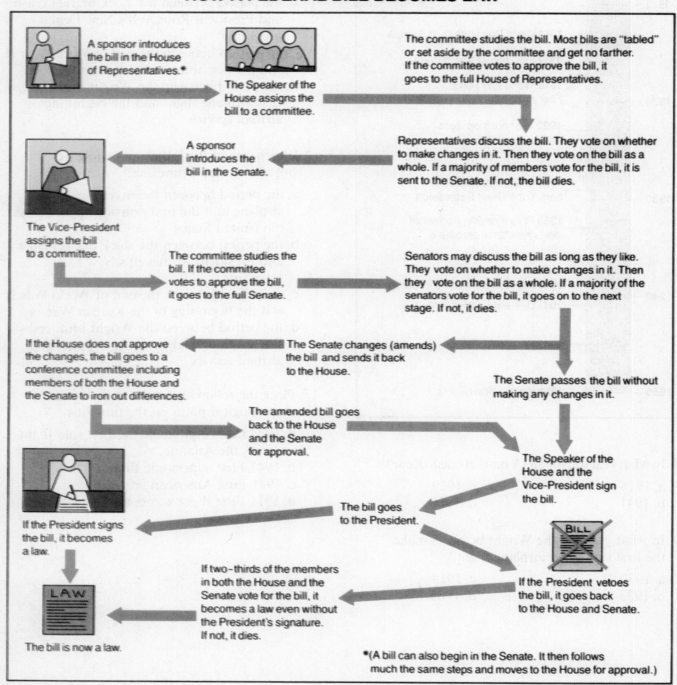

A sponsor introduces the bill in the House of Representatives.*

The Speaker of the House assigns the bill to a committee.

The committee studies the bill. Most bills are "tabled" or set aside by the committee and get no farther. If the committee votes to approve the bill, it goes to the full House of Representatives.

A sponsor introduces the bill in the Senate.

Representatives discuss the bill. They vote on whether to make changes in it. Then they vote on the bill as a whole. If a majority of members vote for the bill, it is sent to the Senate. If not, the bill dies.

The Vice-President assigns the bill to a committee.

The committee studies the bill. If the committee votes to approve the bill, it goes to the full Senate.

Senators may discuss the bill as long as they like. They vote on whether to make changes in it. Then they vote on the bill as a whole. If a majority of the senators vote for the bill, it goes on to the next stage. If not, it dies.

If the House does not approve the changes, the bill goes to a conference committee including members of both the House and the Senate to iron out differences.

The Senate changes (amends) the bill and sends it back to the House.

The Senate passes the bill without making any changes in it.

The amended bill goes back to the House and the Senate for approval.

The Speaker of the House and the Vice-President sign the bill.

If the President signs the bill, it becomes a law.

The bill goes to the President.

If the President vetoes the bill, it goes back to the House and Senate.

LAW

If two-thirds of the members in both the House and the Senate vote for the bill, it becomes a law even without the President's signature. If not, it dies.

The bill is now a law.

*(A bill can also begin in the Senate. It then follows much the same steps and moves to the House for approval.)

1. What is the first step by which a bill becomes a law?

   a. It is sent to the president.
   b. It is assigned to a committee in the House of Representatives.
   c. It is introduced in the House of Representatives or the Senate.
   d. It is sent to a committee in the Senate.

2. What happens to a bill after it passes the house of Congress where it was first introduced?

   a. It is sent back to the original committee for further study.
   b. It is sent to the other house of Congress.
   c. It is sent to the president.
   d. It is sent to the voters.

3. What is the purpose of a conference committee?

   a. to study a bill before it is presented to the House of Representatives
   b. to study a bill before it is presented to the Senate
   c. to sign the bill before it is sent to the president
   d. to work out differences between the House of Representatives and the Senate

4. After a bill is introduced in the Senate, what happens to it next?

   a. It is sent to a committee for study.
   b. Senators vote on it.
   c. It goes to the president.
   d. The vice-president signs it.

5. What happens to a bill that is set aside by the first committee to study it?

   a. It becomes a law.
   b. It goes to the other house of Congress.
   c. It is signed by the president.
   d. It goes no farther unless someone reintroduces it in another session of Congress.

6. How long can the Senate debate a bill?

   a. They can debate it for only one day, unless they take a special vote to debate it longer.
   b. They can debate it for as long as they wish.
   c. They can debate it until the president calls for a vote on it.

7. How many members must vote for the bill if it is to pass the Senate?

   a. all the members who are present
   b. 2/3 of the members who are present
   c. 3/4 of the members who are present
   d. a majority of members who are present

8. When are amendments added to a bill in the House of Representatives?

   a. after the whole House has voted on the bill
   b. before the House votes on the bill
   c. before the bill is sent to committee

9. What can the president do to keep a bill from becoming a law?

   a. amend it          b. sign it          c. veto it

10. If the president vetoes a bill, what happens to the bill next?

    a. It returns to Congress, where it needs to win two thirds of the votes in both the House and the Senate to become law.
    b. It is put on the ballot for the voters to express their opinions.
    c. It returns to congressional committees for further study.

The capitol consists of two wings, hosting meetings of the United States Senate and House of Representatives.

# Reading a Political Cartoon

**Objectives:** to interpret cartoon symbols and identify the main idea of an
editorial cartoon

An **editorial cartoon** expresses an opinion about a public issue. The cartoon may use humor or exaggeration to make a serious point about a law, a political leader, or a public problem. Study the editorial cartoons on these pages and answer the following questions.

The first political cartoon makes a statement about timing. Think about the symbols in the cartoon as you answer the questions about it.

**HERBLOCK'S CARTOON**

"NICE TIMING"

MAIL YOUR INCOME TAX BY APRIL 15 — IRS

25¢ NEW HIGHER RATE FOR SLOWER DELIVERY APRIL 3 U.S. POSTAL "SERVICE"

©1989 HERBLOCK

1. Whom does the person holding the letter represent in this cartoon?

   a. someone who missed the turtle race
   b. a United States taxpayer
   c. the owner of the building where the sign is being posted
   d. a government official

2. What place is represented in this cartoon?

   a. the home of a United States citizen
   b. an office of the Internal Revenue Service
   c. a post office
   d. the state office building

3. Whom does the man putting up the sign represent?

   a. a postal official
   b. the sponsor of the turtle race
   c. a United States taxpayer
   d. the artist who made the sign

4. Who will be most affected by the changes announced in the sign?

   a. taxpayers who mailed their taxes early
   b. taxpayers who mailed their taxes in March
   c. taxpayers who mail their taxes in April

5. What is the main idea of this cartoon?

   a. Posting signs on walls makes citizens angry.
   b. The man with the envelope was going to post a sign in that spot.
   c. The turtle races are going to cost more this year than ever before.
   d. The timing of the higher postal rates will cost taxpayers extra money.

The second editorial cartoon uses the dialogue of the characters in the cartoon to help us understand what problem the cartoonist is calling attention to. Study the cartoon and answer the following questions.

6. Whom do the people in the cartoon represent?

a. highway workers
b. homeless people
c. suburban dwellers

7. What do the buildings in the distance represent?

a. a large, industrial city
b. a large resort area
c. a small rural town
d. a small town along the seacoast

8. What is the main idea of this cartoon?

a. The rivers near large cities are so polluted with chemicals that they will burn.
b. The best way to put out a match is to throw it in the water.
c. The winter is too cold for people to cook meals outside.

9. What is the purpose of the cartoon?

a. to make the reader feel sorry for the people in the cartoon
b. to show the reader the attractions of a large city
c. to remind the reader that many rivers are dangerously polluted

10. What is the author's point-of-view?

a. Poor people in large cities deserve more help.
b. Water pollution is a major problem in urban areas.
c. Large cities have many good sources of heat.

11. Where would you expect to see this cartoon published?

a. in a neighborhood newsletter
b. in a small local newspaper
c. in a large city newspaper

12. Suppose you could use this same cartoon to bring out a problem in your city. On the lines below, write your own dialogue between the characters in the cartoon that would bring out your city's problem. Your dialogue can be completely different than the cartoon here, but should be appropriate for the scene.

_____

_____

_____

_____

_____

_____

# Interpreting Historical Cartoons

**Objectives:** to interpret symbols in historical cartoons and identify the viewpoint that the cartoon expresses

Newspapers and magazines have used cartoons to express ideas for more than 150 years. To understand some historical cartoons, you need a detailed knowledge of history. Other cartoons, however, are easy to understand if you look at them carefully.

The first cartoon was drawn in the late 1800s. At the time, many Americans wanted laws to limit the number of immigrants coming into the United States. Study the cartoon and answer the following questions.

1. Who is the person coming down the gangplank with the pack on his back?

   a. a lawmaker
   b. a new immigrant
   c. a person leaving the United States
   d. a sailor

2. Who are the men standing on the dock?

   a. customs inspectors
   b. sea captains
   c. poor immigrants
   d. wealthy businessmen

3. What message are the men on the dock sending to the man on the gangplank?

   a. "Welcome!"
   b. "Put your hands up!"
   c. "Go back!"

4. What do the shadows behind the men on the dock stand for?

   a. their own background as poor immigrants
   b. poor people who are watching them
   c. other immigrants who would like to come to the United States

5. What is the main idea of this cartoon?

   a. Most Americans want to limit immigration.
   b. All immigrants will get rich in the United States.
   c. There are not enough jobs for immigrants.
   d. People who were once immigrants themselves want to close the door to others.

6. Name two details in the cartoon that would help tell at what time in history this cartoon was drawn, if you didn't know the year.

   _____

   _____

   _____

   _____

This cartoon was drawn in the 1890s. It shows how some of the food producers in the United States felt about banks and other financial institutions. You may want to compare it to the election map for 1896 on page 62. The same issues that divided the country in that election are suggested by this cartoon. Study the cartoon and answer the following questions.

WEST AND SOUTH FEED THE COUNTRY WHILE WALL STREET MILKS IT

7. What does the cow stand for in this cartoon?

    a. one of the national political parties
    b. the economy of the country
    c. a giant animal that will eat up the country

8. Whom do the people feeding the cow represent?

    a. factory workers
    b. business leaders
    c. farmers
    d. bankers and investors

9. What part of the country do the people feeding the cow live in?

    a. the west and south
    b. the east and south
    c. the north and east

10. Whom do the people milking the cow represent?

    a. dairy farmers in the east
    b. the poor and hungry people in the cities
    c. bankers and financiers in eastern cities
    d. political leaders who hope to get votes by helping the farmers

11. What is the artist's point-of-view in this cartoon?

    a. People must cooperate to raise food for the country.
    b. Farmers produce the country's wealth, while bankers get the benefits.
    c. The country should be divided at the Mississippi River.
    d. St. Louis and New York control the economy of the country.

12. Why is the caption important to understanding this cartoon?

    a. It tells the year the cartoon was drawn.
    b. It restates the main idea of the cartoon.
    c. It names the city and state in which the cartoon takes place.

13. Write your own caption for this cartoon that would be appropriate.

_____

_____

_____

_____

# Glossary

**assets** the money and property a person owns

**atlas** a book of maps

**axes** horizontal and vertical lines on a bar graph that show what is being measured or compared

**bar graph** a graph that uses bar shapes to compare amounts

**cardinal directions** the four main directions on a map

**circle graph** (or **pie graph**) a graph that shows a whole divided into parts, to compare amounts

**compass rose** a symbol on a map that shows direction

**continent** one of the seven, large landmasses that covers the Earth

**contour line** line showing all the points of land that have the same elevation

**coordinates** a pair of numbers or letters used to name the exact location of a place on a map

**degree** the unit used to measure latitude and longitude (Each degree is divided into sixty minutes, and each minute is divided into sixty seconds.)

**distortion** change in the size and shape of lands and oceans on a map

**Eastern Hemisphere** the half of the Earth that is east of the Prime Meridian

**elevation** the height of land above sea level

**equator** an imaginary line drawn around the Earth, at 0° latitude

**gazetteer** an index that lists all the place names that appear on maps in an atlas

**GNP (gross national product)** total value of the goods and services that a country produces in a year

**grid** a pattern of criss-cross lines on a map used to help locate places exactly

**historical map** map showing what an area was like during a specific time in history

**intermediate directions** directions that fall between the four cardinal directions

**kilometer** a unit of measure equal to 1,000 meters or about 5/8 of a mile

**line graph** a graph that uses lines to show how amounts have changed or can be compared

**map key** (or **legend**) a list of symbols used on a map and what they mean

**meridians** lines of longitude measuring distance in degrees east and west of the Prime Meridian

**Northern Hemisphere** the half of the Earth that lies north of the equator

**ocean currents** major streams that move constantly through the oceans

**parallels** lines of latitude measuring distance in degrees north and south of the equator

**point-of-view** a person's opinion

**political map** map showing country and state borders, and major cities

**population density** average number of people in an area

**Prime Meridian** an imaginary line drawn from the North to South poles, at 0° longitude

**projection** a way of showing the round Earth on a flat surface

**scale** shows how much distance on Earth is represented by distance on a map

**sea level** the level of the surface of the sea; the starting point for measuring the height and depth of land

**Southern Hemisphere** the half of the Earth that lies south of the equator

**symbol** a picture that represents a thing or idea

**table** data arranged in rows and columns

**time line** a line showing the dates and the order in which certain events happened

**time zone** one of the 24 zones around the world that has the same time throughout the zone

**topography** surface features of land

**Tropic of Cancer** a special line of latitude located 23½° north of the equator

**Tropic of Capricorn** a special line of latitude located 23½° south of the equator

**Western Hemisphere** the half of the Earth that lies west of the Prime Meridian

# Answer Key

## Lesson 1

### pages 2–3

1. east and west
2. NE, SE, SW, NW (clockwise)
3. c
4. c
5. b
6. d
7. c
8. c
9. b
10. a

## Lesson 2

### pages 4–5

1. d
2. c
3. a
4. b
5. d
6. a
7. a
8. b
9. b
10. d
11. on the map of Delaware and Maryland
12. c

## Lesson 3

### pages 6–7

1. d
2. c
3. c
4. d
5. b
6. d
7. b
8. c
9. a
10. a
11. d
12. b
13. d
14. Areas with high population density have more professional sports teams than do areas of low population density.

## Lesson 4

### page 8

1. c
2. See map for answer.
3. a
4. b
5. a. A-2
   b. D-3
   c. E-1
6. d
7. b

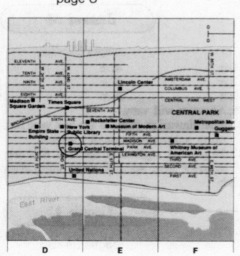

## Lesson 5

### pages 9-11

1. equator
2. South Pole
3. 90° South
4. Prime Meridian
5. a
6. b
7. d
8. c
9. c
10. a
11. c
12. b
13. d
14. b
15. b
16. a
17. b
18. b
19. a. Denver
    b. Columbus
    c. Indianapolis
20. a. 45° N, 123° W
    b. 45° N, 93° W
    c. 39° N, 120° W
    d. 36° N, 79° W

## Lesson 6

### pages 12–13

**Alaska**

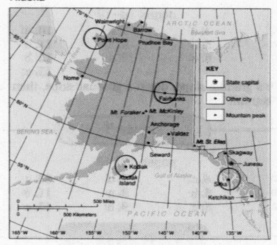

1. c
2. b
3. d
4. d
5. c
6. a
7. b
8. c
9. c
10. c
11. b
12. b
13. d
14. a
15. b
16. a. Ketchikan
    b. Nome
    c. Seward
17. a. 57° N, 135° W
    b. 65° N, 148° W
    c. 58° N, 152° W
    d. 68° N, 167° W
18. See map for answers.

## Lesson 7

### pages 14–15

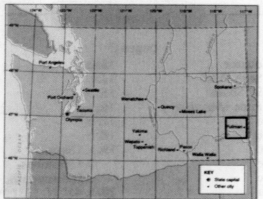

1. a
2. c
3. a
4. b
5. b
6. c
7. c
8. See map for answer.
9. a
10. 47°30′ N, 122° 30′ W
11. 47°36′ N, 122°20′ W
12. c
13. a
14. Quincy

## Lesson 8

### pages 16–17

| | | | |
|---|---|---|---|
| 1. c | 4. d | 7. a | 10. d |
| 2. a | 5. b | 8. c | 11. b |
| 3. c | 6. c | 9. a | 12. b |
| | | | 13. c |

14. up a gradual slope, down a gradual slope, then up a steep hill

## Lesson 9

### pages 18–19

| | | | |
|---|---|---|---|
| 1. c | 4. c | 7. d | 10. c |
| 2. b | 5. b | 8. a | 11. b |
| 3. a | 6. c | 9. b | 12. c |

## Lesson 10

### pages 20–21

| | | | |
|---|---|---|---|
| 1. b | 3. b | 5. a | 7. c |
| 2. a | 4. d | 6. a | 8. a |

9. World map shows the larger area.

## Lesson 11

### pages 22–23

| | | |
|---|---|---|
| 1. b | 6. b | 11. a. ahead-one |
| 2. c | 7. b | b. back-one |
| 3. c | 8. c | c. back-two |
| 4. a | 9. d | d. ahead-two |
| 5. d | 10. d | e. ahead-one |

## Lesson 12

### pages 24–25

| | | | |
|---|---|---|---|
| 1. a | 4. c | 7. c | 10. a |
| 2. b | 5. d | 8. a | 11. b |
| 3. c | 6. c | 9. b | 12. b |

## Lesson 13

### pages 26–27

| | | | |
|---|---|---|---|
| 1. c | 4. b | 7. a | 10. b |
| 2. a | 5. d | 8. c | 11. d |
| 3. b | 6. b | 9. d | |

12. Sample answer: Go east on Camelback Rd. about 1 mile to Interstate 17. Go about 4.5 miles south to Van Buren St. Go east on Van Buren St. about 9 miles until it becomes Mill Ave. Follow Mill Ave. about 2 miles.

## Lesson 14

### pages 28–29

| | | | |
|---|---|---|---|
| 1. d | 5. a | 9. d | 13. c |
| 2. d | 6. c | 10. b | 14. c |
| 3. b | 7. c | 11. a | |
| 4. c | 8. a | 12. b | |

15. Answers could include expanding area, river, traffic and others.

## Lesson 15

### pages 30–31

| | | | |
|---|---|---|---|
| 1. b | 5. d | 9. a | 13. b |
| 2. a | 6. d | 10. b | 14. d |
| 3. a | 7. c | 11. b | 15. c |
| 4. c | 8. b | 12. d | |

## Lesson 16

### pages 32–33

| | | |
|---|---|---|
| 1. c | 4. d | 7. d |
| 2. c | 5. c | 8. d |
| 3. b | 6. a | 9. c |

10. Answers will vary.
11. The Hawaiian Islands are hot year round with one rainy season and one dry season.
12. In general, regions of the U.S. that are closer to the equator have warmer, more rainy climates.
13. b

## Lesson 17

### pages 34–35

| | | |
|---|---|---|
| 1. c | 4. a | 7. c |
| 2. c | 5. c | 8. St. Louis |
| 3. b | 6. c | 9. snowy weather |

10. Answer should include types of rain clothes.
11. b
12. Answers will vary.

## Lesson 18

pages 36–37

| | | | |
|---|---|---|---|
| 1. a | 5. c | 9. b | 13. d |
| 2. d | 6. b | 10. b | 14. c |
| 3. b | 7. c | 11. d | |
| 4. d | 8. d | 12. b | |

## Lesson 19

pages 38–39

| | | | |
|---|---|---|---|
| 1. a | 4. a | 7. c | 10. b |
| 2. c | 5. b | 8. d | 11. d |
| 3. d | 6. a | 9. a | 12. a |

## Lesson 20

pages 40–41

| | | |
|---|---|---|
| 1. a | 4. c | 7. a |
| 2. c | 5. b | 8. c |
| 3. b | 6. b | 9. b |
| | | 10. b |

11. Answers could include Lee would head south, avoid Union troops, or choose a route near his headquarters.

## Lesson 21

page 42

1. Answers may vary.
2. Sample answers:
   A: proximity to highways
   B: mountain scenery
   C: proximity to the river, the railroad, and the highway
   D: proximity of farm land
   Other answers are possible.

| | | |
|---|---|---|
| 3. a | 5. d | 7. c |
| 4. c | 6. b | 8. b |

## Lesson 22

page 43

1. Answers may vary.
2. Sample answers:
   D: proximity to the sea and highway
   F: proximity to the sea and highway
   E: proximity to the sea, and the highway
   B: sheltered location and the access to the sea by river
   Other answers are also possible.

| | | |
|---|---|---|
| 3. a | 5. d | 7. b |
| 4. b | 6. d | 8. c |

## Lesson 23

pages 44–45

| | | |
|---|---|---|
| 1. b | 6. a | 11. b |
| 2. c | 7. Answers will | 12. d |
| 3. b | vary. | 13. c |
| 4. c | 8. b | 14. b |
| 5. a | 9. a | 15. d |
| | 10. a | |

## Lesson 24

pages 46–47

| | | |
|---|---|---|
| 1. b | 4. a | 7. c |
| 2. c | 5. d | 8. b |
| 3. c | 6. b | 9. d |

10. Student's route should begin at Hannibal, Missouri, and also include New Salem, Springfield, and Charleston, Illinois. Criteria used to choose routes could include shortest distance, main roads, scenic roads, etc.

## Lesson 25

pages 48–49

| | | |
|---|---|---|
| 1. b | 4. b | 7. b |
| 2. a | 5. c | 8. a |
| 3. a | 6. d | 9. c |

10. Student's route should begin at Las Cruces. The most direct route from there is to go northeast on Highway 70 and 82 through White Sands National Monument. After White Sands, the route should follow Route 82 east to Artesia. At Artesia, the route turns south on Route 285 to Carlsbad and the Living Desert. Then the route turns southwest on Route 62 and 180 to the Carlsbad Caverns.

## Lesson 26

page 50

| | | | |
|---|---|---|---|
| 1. d | 3. c | 5. d | 7. b |
| 2. a | 4. b | 6. b | |

## Lesson 27

page 51

| | | |
|---|---|---|
| 1. a | 2. c | 3. b |

4. Sample answers for point C:
   a. The new lake would be close to both towns for recreational use.
   b. The river has a natural bend at point C.
   c. The farm land south of C would be protected by the dam.
5. a

## Lesson 28

pages 52–53

| | | | |
|---|---|---|---|
| 1. b | 5. d | 9. d | 13. b |
| 2. a | 6. b | 10. b | 14. a |
| 3. c | 7. b | 11. c | |
| 4. a | 8. c | 12. c | |

## Lesson 29

page 54

| | | | |
|---|---|---|---|
| 1. b | 3. d | 5. a | 7. c |
| 2. c | 4. d | 6. b | 8. a |

## Lesson 30

page 55

| | | | |
|---|---|---|---|
| 1. b | 3. d | 5. c | 7. d |
| 2. c | 4. c | 6. b | 8. a |

## Lesson 31

page 56

| | | | |
|---|---|---|---|
| 1. a | 3. b | 5. b | 7. d |
| 2. a | 4. d | 6. d | |

## Lesson 32

page 57

| | | |
|---|---|---|
| 1. b | 3. b | 5. d |
| 2. c | 4. c | 6. d |

## Lesson 33

page 58

| | | | |
|---|---|---|---|
| 1. c | 3. c | 5. b | 7. b |
| 2. a | 4. c | 6. a | 8. d |

## Lesson 34

page 59

| | | | |
|---|---|---|---|
| 1. c | 3. a | 5. c | 7. a |
| 2. b | 4. c | 6. a | 8. b |

## Lesson 35

pages 60–61

| | | | |
|---|---|---|---|
| 1. b | 4. a | 7. d | 10. b |
| 2. d | 5. b | 8. c | 11. c |
| 3. a | 6. b | 9. a | 12. a |

## Lesson 36

pages 62–63

| | | | |
|---|---|---|---|
| 1. c | 4. a | 7. c | 10. b |
| 2. b | 5. b | 8. b | 11. c |
| 3. d | 6. c | 9. d | 12. a |
| | | | 13. c |

## Lesson 37

pages 64–65

| | | | |
|---|---|---|---|
| 1. c | 5. a | 9. c | 13. c |
| 2. b | 6. c | 10. a | 14. d |
| 3. d | 7. b | 11. d | 15. b |
| 4. c | 8. b | 12. d | |

## Lesson 38

pages 66–67

| | | | |
|---|---|---|---|
| 1. c | 5. c | 9. c | 13. a |
| 2. b | 6. a | 10. d | 14. b |
| 3. b | 7. c | 11. b | 15. c |
| 4. d | 8. c | 12. c | 16. a |

## Lesson 39

pages 68–69

1. d
2. a
3. c
4. b
5. c
6. c
7. d
8. c
9. d
10. b
11. b
12. a
13. See time line for answers.

1900
1903 Wright brothers make the first successful airplane flight.
1910
d.
1914 World War I begins in Europe.
1917 U.S. enters World War I.
1918 World War I ends. First airmail service in U.S.
1920
1923 First nonstop flight across the U.S.
a.
1929 Stock market crash begins the Great Depression.
1930
1933 Pres. Franklin Roosevelt starts New Deal programs.
1940
1939 World War II begins in Europe.
c.
1941 U.S. enters World War II.
1945 World War II ends.
b.
1950
1950 Korean War begins.

## Lesson 40

pages 70–71

| | | | |
|---|---|---|---|
| 1. c | 4. a | 7. d | 10. a |
| 2. b | 5. d | 8. b | |
| 3. d | 6. b | 9. c | |

## Lesson 41

pages 72–73

| | | | |
|---|---|---|---|
| 1. b | 4. c | 7. a | 10. b |
| 2. c | 5. d | 8. a | 11. c |
| 3. a | 6. b | 9. c | 12. Answers will vary. |

## Lesson 42

pages 74–75

| | | |
|---|---|---|
| 1. b | 3. c | 5. d |
| 2. d | 4. a | |

6. Answers could include: the style of clothing, travel by ship, style of luggage.

| | | |
|---|---|---|
| 7. b | 10. c | 13. Answers may vary. |
| 8. c | 11. b | |
| 9. a | 12. b | |

# ATLAS

## CONTENTS

| | |
|---|---|
| *The World* | 82-83 |
| *North America* | 84 |
| *South America* | 85 |
| *Europe* | 86 |
| *Asia* | 87 |
| *Africa* | 88 |
| *Australia and the South Pacific* | 89 |
| *United States* | 90-91 |
| *Canada* | 92 |
| *Mexico* | 92 |

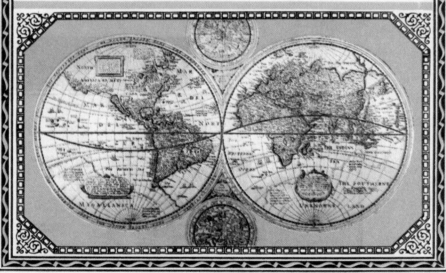

NORTH
AMERICA

*ARCTIC OCEAN*

ALASKA
(U.S.)

CANADA

Aleutian
Islands
(U.S.)

Ottawa ★

Washington, D.C. ★

*NORTH PACIFIC OCEAN*

UNITED STATES

BERMUDA (U.K.)

Tropic of Cancer

MEXICO

Hawaii
(U.S.)

Mexico City ★  Belmopan ★ BELIZE
GUATEMALA  HONDURAS (see inset)
Guatemala City ★ ★ Tegucigalpa
EL SALVADOR ★ NICARAGUA
San Salvador  Managua ★
COSTA RICA ★ ★ San José  Caracas ★
PANAMA  Panama City ★ VENEZUELA  GUYANA
Bogotá ★  Georgetown ★
COLOMBIA  Paramar

Equator

Galápagos Is.  Quito ★
(Ecuador)  ECUADOR

SOUTH
AMERICA

PERU

Lima ★

BRAZ

Brasília ★

BOLIVIA
La Paz ★
Sucre ★

20°S

Tropic of Capricorn

PARAGUAY

São P

Asunción ★

CHILE

URU

Santiago ★  Buenos
Aires ★  Mo

ARGENTINA

*SOUTH PACIFIC OCEAN*

40°S

60°S

Antarctic Circle

**ANTARCTICA**

## WORLD
★ National capital

---

**INSET**

Florida

GULF OF
MEXICO

*ATLANTIC OCEAN*

Nassau ★
THE
BAHAMAS

0        200      400 Miles
0      200    400 Kilometers

Tropic of Cancer

Havana ★

CUBA

20°N

N

HAITI  DOMINICAN
REPUBLIC  PUERTO RICO
(U.S.)  VIRGIN ISLANDS
(U.K. & U.S.)

JAMAICA  Port-au-Prince ★ ★  Santo
★  Domingo  San Juan  ANTIGUA & BARBUDA

Kingston

GUADELOUPE (FR.)

DOMINICA

MARTINIQUE

*CARIBBEAN SEA*  ST. LUCIA

ST. VINCENT &  BARBADOS
THE GRENADINES

GRENADA

TRINIDAD
AND TOBAGO  10°N

---

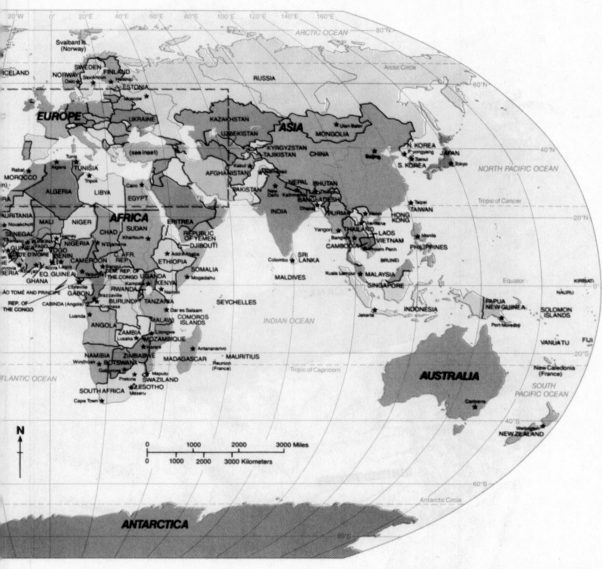

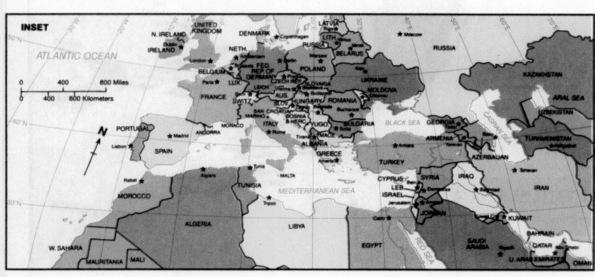

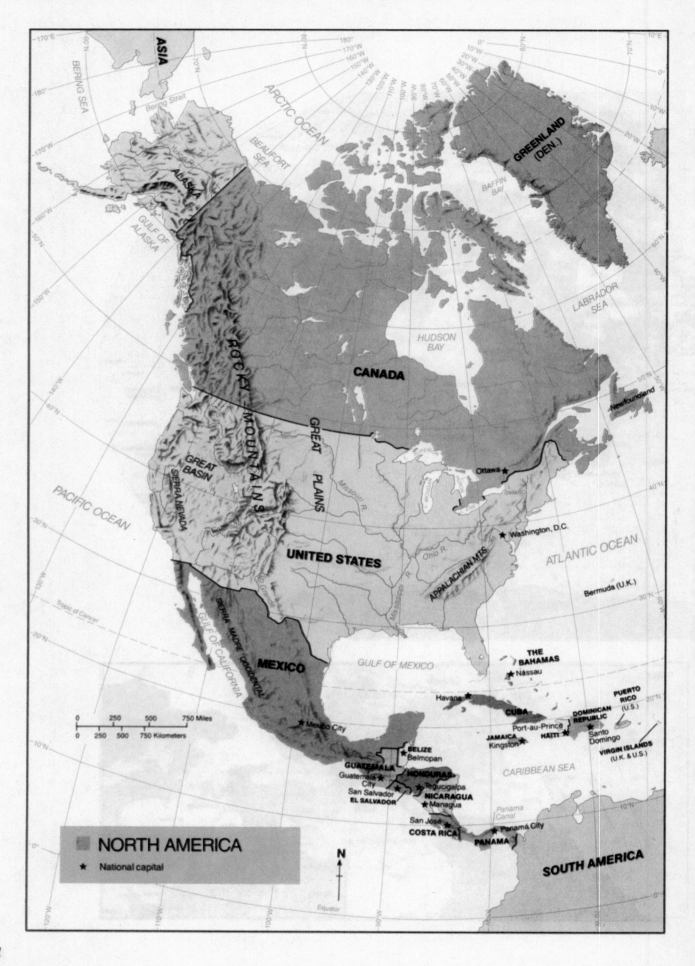

NORTH AMERICA

★ National capital

SOUTH AMERICA

★ National capital

NORTH AMERICA

CARIBBEAN SEA

Caracas

VENEZUELA

Orinoco R.

Georgetown

GUYANA

Paramaribo

Bogotá

GUIANA-HIGHLANDS

Cayenne

COLOMBIA

SURINAME

FRENCH GUIANA

Galápagos Islands (E.C.)

Quito

ECUADOR

Equator

AMAZON

Negro R.

Amazon R.

BASIN

PERU

Madeira R.

BRAZIL

PACIFIC OCEAN

Lima

La Paz

BOLIVIA

Sucre

São Francisco R.

Brasília

BRAZILIAN HIGHLANDS

Paraguay R.

GRAN CHACO

CHILE

PARAGUAY

Tropic of Capricorn

Asunción

ATLANTIC OCEAN

Paraná R.

N

ARGENTINA

Santiago

PAMPAS

URUGUAY

Buenos Aires

Montevideo

PATAGONIA

0   200   400   600 Miles

0   200   400   600 Kilometers

Strait of Magellan

Falkland Islands (U.K.)

Tierra Del Fuego

South Georgia Island (U.K.)

Cape Horn

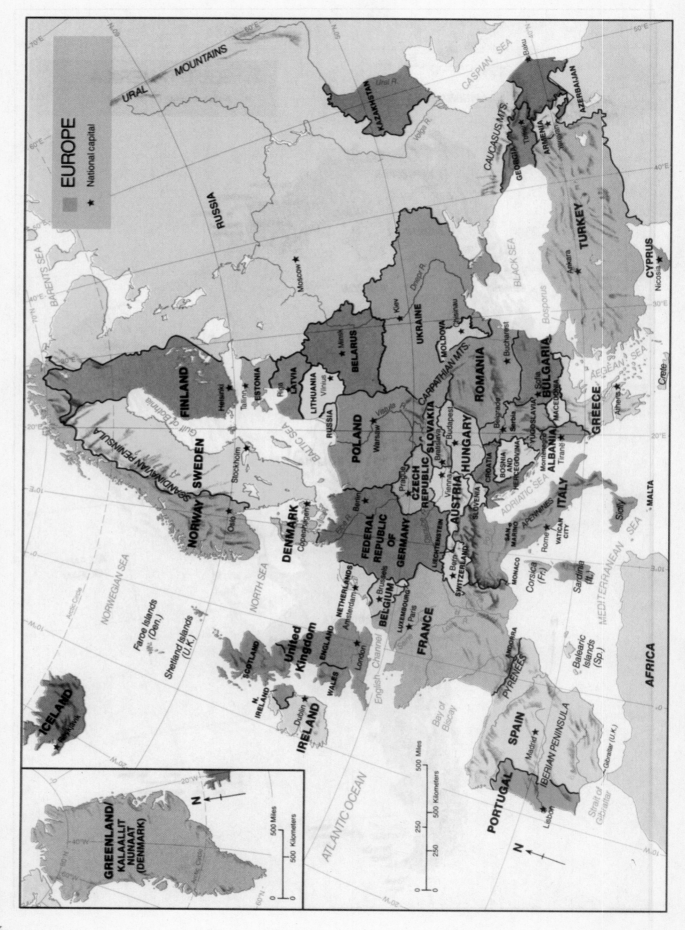

EUROPE

★ National capital

URAL MOUNTAINS

KAZAKHSTAN

Ural R.

Volga R.

CASPIAN SEA

Baku ★

AZERBAIJAN

ARMENIA
Yerevan ★

Tbilisi ★
GEORGIA

CAUCASUS MTS.

RUSSIA

BARENTS SEA

Moscow ★

Kiev ★

UKRAINE

Dnepr R.

Chisinau ★
MOLDOVA

BLACK SEA

Bucharest ★
ROMANIA

CARPATHIAN MTS.

TURKEY

Ankara ★

Bosporus

AEGEAN SEA

GREECE

Athens ★

CYPRUS
Nicosia ★

Crete

FINLAND

Helsinki ★

Tallinn ★
ESTONIA

Riga ★
LATVIA

Vilnius ★
LITHUANIA

Minsk ★
BELARUS

Sofia ★
BULGARIA

MACEDONIA

Gulf of Bothnia

SCANDINAVIAN PENINSULA

SWEDEN

Stockholm ★

RUSSIA

BALTIC SEA

POLAND

Warsaw ★

Vistula

Belgrade ★
Serbia

YUGOSLAVIA

Tiranë ★
ALBANIA

ADRIATIC SEA

Budapest ★
HUNGARY

SLOVAKIA

Bratislava ★

CZECH REPUBLIC

Prague ★

Vienna ★
AUSTRIA

CROATIA

SLOVENIA

BOSNIA AND HERCEGOVINA

Montenegro

APENNINES

ITALY

Rome ★
VATICAN CITY

NORWAY

Oslo ★

DENMARK

Copenhagen ★

Berlin ★
Elbe R.

FEDERAL REPUBLIC OF GERMANY

Danube R.

LIECHTENSTEIN

Bern ★
SWITZERLAND

SAN MARINO

MONACO

Corsica (Fr.)

Sardinia (It.)

MEDITERRANEAN SEA

Sicily

MALTA

NORWEGIAN SEA

NORTH SEA

NETHERLANDS
Amsterdam ★

Brussels ★
BELGIUM

LUXEMBOURG

Paris ★
Seine

FRANCE

ANDORRA

PYRENEES

Balearic Islands (Sp.)

AFRICA

Arctic Circle

Faroe Islands (Den.)

Shetland Islands (U.K.)

SCOTLAND

United Kingdom

ENGLAND

London ★

WALES

English Channel

Bay of Biscay

SPAIN

Madrid ★

IBERIAN PENINSULA

Gibraltar (U.K.)

Strait of Gibraltar

ICELAND

Reykjavik ★

N. IRELAND

Dublin ★
IRELAND

ATLANTIC OCEAN

PORTUGAL

Lisbon ★

500 Miles

500 Kilometers

250

250

500 Miles

500 Kilometers

N

GREENLAND/ KALAALLIT NUNAAT (DENMARK)

Arctic Circle

N

86

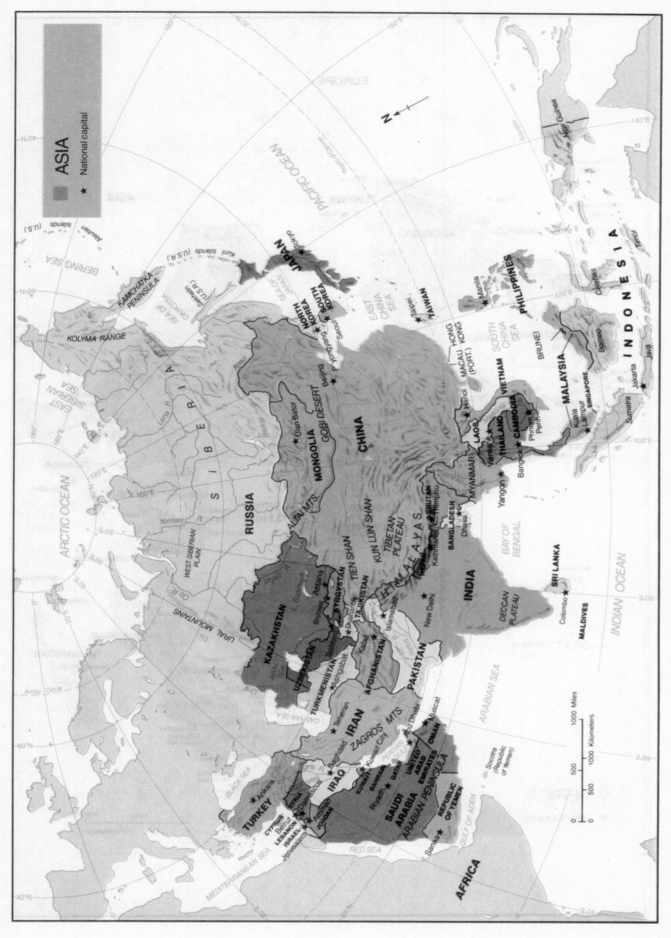

ASIA

★ National capital

EUROPE

PACIFIC OCEAN

Tropic of Cancer

N

New Guinea

140°E

ARCTIC OCEAN

Aleutian
Islands (U.S.)

BERING SEA

Kuril Islands (U.S.R.)

Sakhalin (U.S.R.)

KAMCHATKA
PENINSULA

KOLYMA RANGE

SEA OF
OKHOTSK

SEA OF
JAPAN

JAPAN

Tokyo ★

NORTH
KOREA

SOUTH
KOREA

EAST
CHINA
SEA

TAIWAN

Taipei ★

PHILIPPINES

Manila ★

120°E

INDONESIA

Timor

Equator

EAST
SIBERIAN
SEA

S I B E R I A

Lena R.

Baikal

Pyongyang ★

Seoul ★

HONG
KONG

MACAU
(PORT.)

VIETNAM

SOUTH
CHINA
SEA

BRUNEI

Borneo

Celebes

Jakarta ★

Java

ARCTIC OCEAN

Arctic Circle

Yenisey R.

WEST SIBERIAN
PLAIN

URAL MOUNTAINS

Ob R.

RUSSIA

Ulan Bator ★

MONGOLIA

GOBI DESERT

Beijing ★

CHINA

ALTAI MTS.

TIEN SHAN

KUN LUN SHAN

TIBETAN
PLATEAU

H I M A L A Y A S

Hanoi ★

LAOS

Vientiane ★

THAILAND

Bangkok ★

CAMBODIA

Phnom
Penh ★

MYANMAR

Yangon ★

MALAYSIA

Kuala
Lumpur ★

SINGAPORE

Sumatra

KAZAKHSTAN

L. Balkhash

Astana ★

UZBEKISTAN

KYRGYZSTAN

Bishkek ★

Tashkent ★

TAJIKISTAN

Dushanbe ★

ARAL
SEA

TURKMENISTAN

Ashgabat ★

Kabul ★

AFGHANISTAN

Islamabad ★

PAKISTAN

Kashgar

Indus R.

Thimphu ★

BHUTAN

NEPAL

Kathmandu ★

BANGLADESH

Dhaka ★

INDIA

New Delhi ★

DECCAN
PLATEAU

BAY OF
BENGAL

SRI LANKA

Colombo ★

MALDIVES

INDIAN OCEAN

80°E

CASPIAN SEA

Tehran ★

IRAN

ZAGROS MTS.

Baghdad ★

IRAQ

Kuwait ★

KUWAIT

Riyadh ★

SAUDI
ARABIA

BAHRAIN

QATAR

Abu Dhabi ★

UNITED
ARAB
EMIRATES

OMAN

Muscat ★

ARABIAN
PENINSULA

ARABIAN SEA

Socotra
(Republic
of Yemen)

URAL R.

Volga R.

BLACK SEA

Ankara ★

TURKEY

CYPRUS

SYRIA

LEBANON

Beirut ★

Damascus ★

ISRAEL

Jerusalem ★

Amman ★

JORDAN

Tigris R.

Euphrates R.

PERSIAN GULF

REPUBLIC
OF YEMEN

Sanaa ★

GULF OF ADEN

RED SEA

MEDITERRANEAN SEA

AFRICA

Tropic of Cancer

1000 Miles

1000 Kilometers

500

500

0

0

60°N

40°N

40°N

60°N

30°N

30°S

180°

160°E

140°E

120°E

100°E

80°E

60°N

87

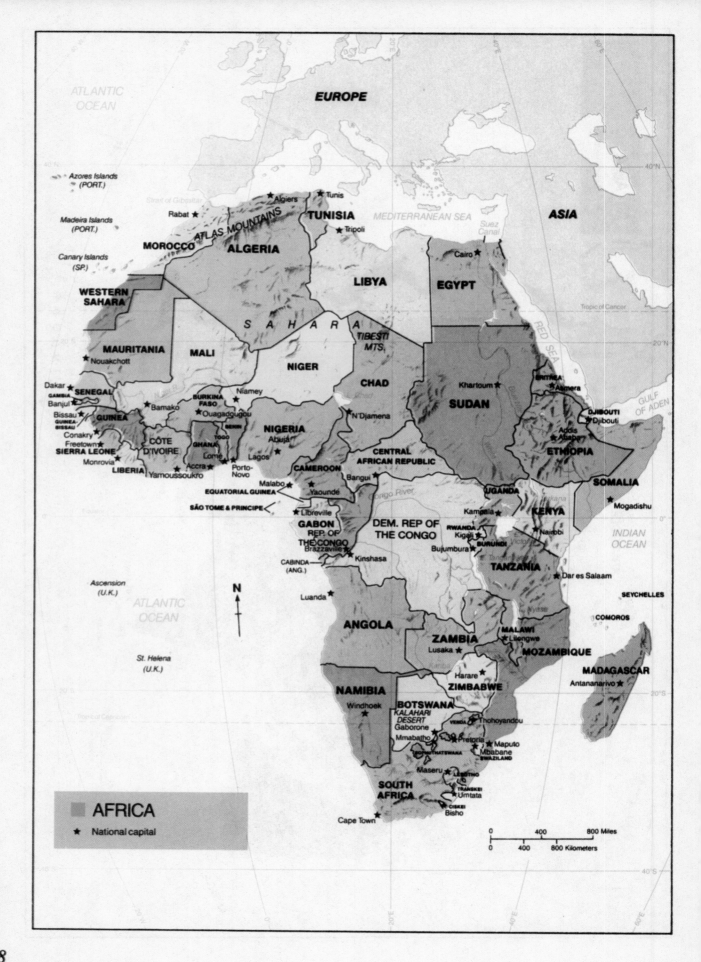

ATLANTIC
OCEAN

EUROPE

*Azores Islands
(PORT.)*

*Madeira Islands
(PORT.)*

MEDITERRANEAN SEA

ASIA

*Canary Islands
(SP.)*

Strait of Gibraltar

★ Algiers
★ Tunis

Rabat ★

**TUNISIA**

Suez
Canal

ATLAS MOUNTAINS

★ Tripoli

Cairo ★

**MOROCCO**

**ALGERIA**

**LIBYA**

**EGYPT**

**WESTERN
SAHARA**

Tropic of Cancer

S A H A R A

**MAURITANIA**

TIBESTI
MTS.

RED SEA

Nouakchott ★

**MALI**

**NIGER**

Khartoum ★

ERITREA
★ Asmera

Dakar ★
GAMBIA
Banjul ★

**SENEGAL**

Niamey ★

**CHAD**

**SUDAN**

**DJIBOUTI**
Djibouti ★

GULF
OF ADEN

Bissau ★
GUINEA-
BISSAU

**GUINEA**

Bamako ★

**BURKINA
FASO**
Ouagadougou ★

N'Djamena ★

Addis
Ababa ★

Conakry ★
Freetown ★

BENIN

**NIGERIA**
Abuja ★

**ETHIOPIA**

**SIERRA LEONE**

**CÔTE
D'IVOIRE**

GHANA
Lomé
TOGO

**CENTRAL
AFRICAN REPUBLIC**

**SOMALIA**

Monrovia ★

**LIBERIA**
Yamoussoukro ★

Accra ★

Porto-
Novo ★

Lagos ★

**CAMEROON**

Bangui ★

Congo River

**UGANDA**

★ Mogadishu

Malabo ★

**EQUATORIAL GUINEA**

★
Yaoundé

Kampala ★

**KENYA**

INDIAN
OCEAN

**SÃO TOMÉ & PRINCIPE**

★ Libreville

Equator

**GABON**

**DEM. REP OF
THE CONGO**

RWANDA
Kigali ★

Nairobi ★

**SEYCHELLES**

*Ascension
(U.K.)*

ATLANTIC
OCEAN

**REP. OF
THE CONGO**
Brazzaville ★

BURUNDI
Bujumbura ★

**COMOROS**

CABINDA
(ANG.)

Kinshasa ★

**TANZANIA**

★ Dar es Salaam

*St. Helena
(U.K.)*

Luanda ★

**ANGOLA**

**MALAWI**
★ Lilongwe

**ZAMBIA**

**MADAGASCAR**

Lusaka ★

**MOZAMBIQUE**

Harare ★

Antananarivo ★

**NAMIBIA**

**ZIMBABWE**

Windhoek ★

**BOTSWANA**
*KALAHARI
DESERT*
Gaborone ★

VENDA
Thohoyandou

Tropic of Capricorn

Mmabatho ★
BOPHUTHATSWANA

★ Pretoria

★ Maputo
Mbabane ★
SWAZILAND

Maseru ★
LESOTHO

**SOUTH
AFRICA**

TRANSKEI
Umtata ★

CISKEI
Bisho ★

Cape Town ★

N

|   | AFRICA |
|---|---|
| ★ | National capital |

| 0 | 400 | 800 Miles |
|---|---|---|
| 0 | 400 | 800 Kilometers |

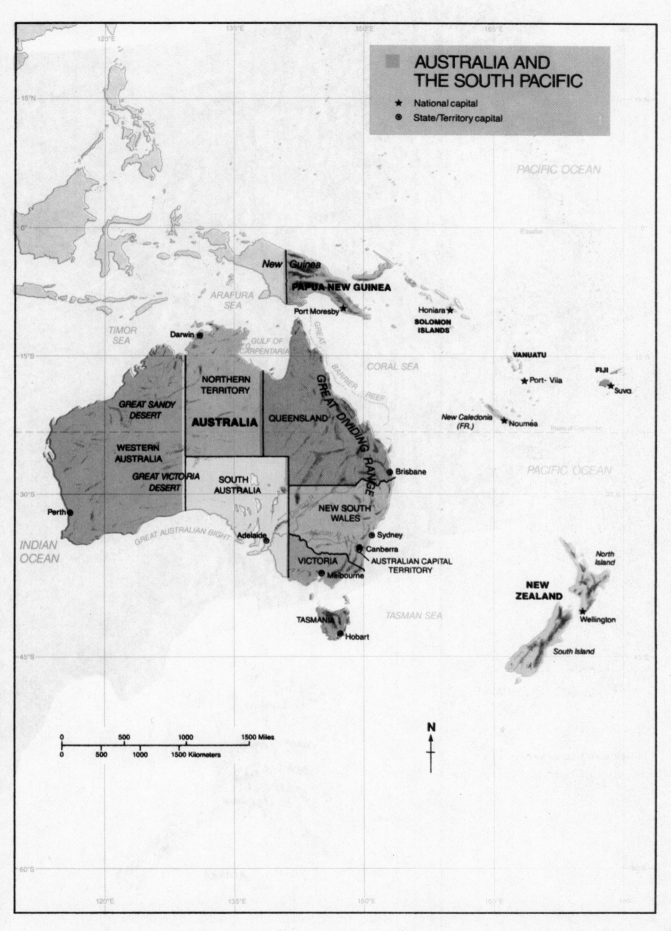

**AUSTRALIA AND THE SOUTH PACIFIC**

★ National capital
◉ State/Territory capital

PACIFIC OCEAN

Equator

*New Guinea*
**PAPUA NEW GUINEA**
Port Moresby ★

Honiara ★
**SOLOMON ISLANDS**

*ARAFURA SEA*

*TIMOR SEA*

Darwin ◉

*GULF OF CARPENTARIA*

*CORAL SEA*

**VANUATU**
★ Port- Vila

**FIJI**
★ Suva

NORTHERN TERRITORY

*GREAT SANDY DESERT*

**AUSTRALIA**

QUEENSLAND

*GREAT DIVIDING RANGE*

New Caledonia (FR.)
★ Nouméa

*Tropic of Capricorn*

**WESTERN AUSTRALIA**

*GREAT VICTORIA DESERT*

**SOUTH AUSTRALIA**

Brisbane

PACIFIC OCEAN

Perth ◉

**NEW SOUTH WALES**

*GREAT AUSTRALIAN BIGHT*

Adelaide ◉

Sydney ◉
Canberra ◉
**AUSTRALIAN CAPITAL TERRITORY**

*INDIAN OCEAN*

*Murray R.*

**VICTORIA**
Melbourne ◉

**NEW ZEALAND**

*North Island*

**TASMANIA**
Hobart ◉

*TASMAN SEA*

Wellington ★

*South Island*

N

0      500      1000      1500 Miles
0    500    1000    1500 Kilometers

*BARRIER REEF*

UNITED STATES

- ★ National capital
- ◉ State capital
- • Other city

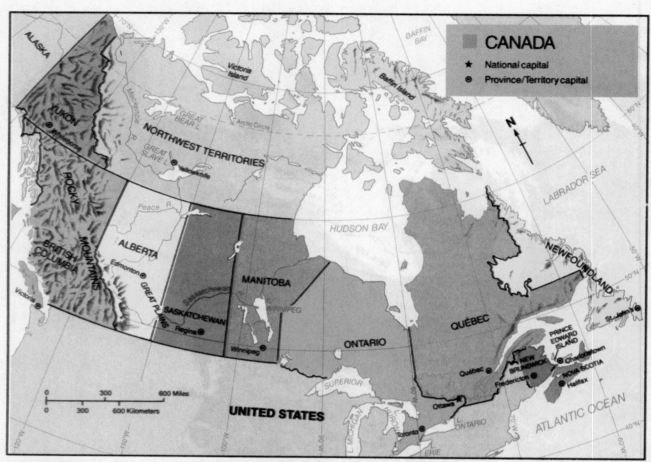

### CANADA

- ★ National capital
- ⊙ Province/Territory capital

ALASKA

YUKON
Whitehorse ⊙

NORTHWEST TERRITORIES

Victoria Island

GREAT BEAR L.

Arctic Circle

Mackenzie R.

GREAT SLAVE L.
Yellowknife ⊙

BAFFIN BAY

Baffin Island

ROCKY MOUNTAINS

BRITISH COLUMBIA

Peace R.

ALBERTA

GREAT PLAINS

Edmonton ⊙

Saskatchewan R.

SASKATCHEWAN
Regina ⊙

Victoria ⊙

MANITOBA

WINNIPEG

Winnipeg ⊙

ONTARIO

HUDSON BAY

LABRADOR SEA

NEWFOUNDLAND

QUÉBEC

PRINCE EDWARD ISLAND
Charlottetown ⊙

St. John's ⊙

Québec ⊙

NEW BRUNSWICK
Fredericton ⊙

NOVA SCOTIA
Halifax ⊙

SUPERIOR

L. MICHIGAN

L. HURON

Ottawa ★

ATLANTIC OCEAN

ONTARIO

Toronto ⊙

ERIE

N

300    600 Miles
300    600 Kilometers

**UNITED STATES**

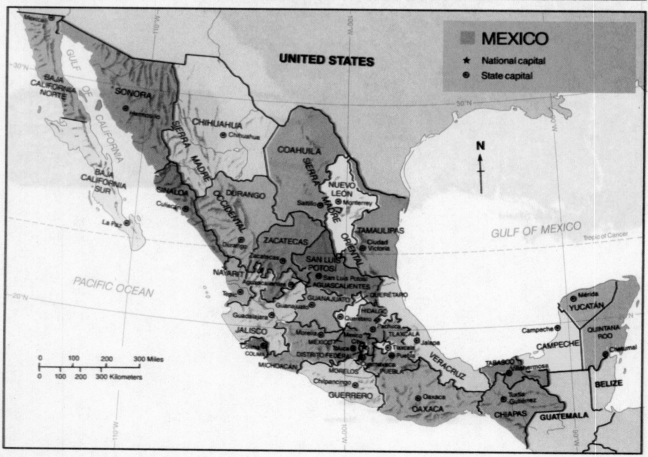

### MEXICO

- ★ National capital
- ⊙ State capital

**UNITED STATES**

Mexicali ⊙

GULF OF CALIFORNIA

BAJA CALIFORNIA NORTE

SONORA
Hermosillo ⊙

CALIFORNIA

CHIHUAHUA
Chihuahua ⊙

COAHUILA

BAJA CALIFORNIA SUR

SIERRA MADRE OCCIDENTAL

SINALOA
Culiacán ⊙

La Paz ⊙

DURANGO
Durango ⊙

SIERRA MADRE ORIENTAL

NUEVO LEÓN
Saltillo ⊙    Monterrey ⊙

ZACATECAS
Zacatecas ⊙

TAMAULIPAS
Ciudad Victoria ⊙

GULF OF MEXICO

Tropic of Cancer

PACIFIC OCEAN

SAN LUIS POTOSÍ
San Luis Potosí ⊙

NAYARIT
Tepic ⊙

AGUASCALIENTES
Aguascalientes ⊙

GUANAJUATO
Guanajuato ⊙

QUERÉTARO

HIDALGO
Pachuca ⊙

MÉRIDA ⊙
YUCATÁN

JALISCO
Guadalajara ⊙

Querétaro ⊙

TLAXCALA
Tlaxcala ⊙

Campeche ⊙

QUINTANA ROO

COLIMA
Colima ⊙

MICHOACÁN
Morelia ⊙

MÉXICO
Toluca ⊙

Mexico City ★

DISTRITO FEDERAL

MORELOS
Cuernavaca ⊙

PUEBLA
Puebla ⊙

Jalapa ⊙

VERACRUZ

CAMPECHE

TABASCO
Villahermosa ⊙

Chetumal ⊙

BELIZE

Chilpancingo ⊙

GUERRERO

OAXACA
Oaxaca ⊙

CHIAPAS
Tuxtla Gutiérrez ⊙

GUATEMALA

N

100    200    300 Miles
100    200    300 Kilometers